Orthodox Pastoral Service

Books by William C. Mills

Pastoral Ministry

Church, World, and Kingdom: The Eucharistic Foundations of Alexander Schmemann's Pastoral Theology

Kyprian Kern: Orthodox Pastoral Service

Called to Serve: Readings on Ministry From the Orthodox Church

Church and World: Essays in Honor of Michael Plekon

Biblical Prayer and Spirituality

A 30 Day Retreat: A Personal Guide to Spiritual Renewa

Walking with God: Stories of Life and Faith

Come Follow Me

The Prayer of St. Ephrem: A Biblical Commentary

Our Father: A Prayer for Christian Living

Encountering Jesus in the Gospels

Lectionary Series

A Light to the Gentiles: Reflections on the Gospel of Luke

Baptize All Nations: Reflections on the Gospel of Matthew for the Pentecostal Season

Feasts of Faith: Reflections on the Major Feast Days

From Pascha to Pentecost: Reflections on the Gospel of John

Let Us Attend: Reflections on the Gospel of Mark for the Lenten Season

Prepare O Bethlehem: Reflections on the Scripture Readings for the Christmas-Epiphany Season

ORTHODOX PASTORAL SERVICE

ARCHIMANDRITE KYPRIAN KERN

Translated by Mary Goddard
Edited with an Introduction by William C. Mills

First Published by Orthodox Research Institute, 2009
Reprinted by OCABS Press, 2018

Originally published in Russian as *Православное пастырское служение*, Paris, 1957. Thank you to V. Rev. Boris Bobrinskoy and the Institut de Théologie Orthodoxe Saint-Serge for granting permission to translate and publish this book.

Cover photograph provided courtesy of St. Gregory the Theologian Orthodox Church, Wappingers Falls, NY.

© 2009 William C. Mills

All rights reserved. No part of this publication may be reproduced or transmitted in any form or by any means, electronic or mechanical, in- cluding photocopying, recording, or any information storage and retriev- al system, without permission in writing from the author or publisher.

ISBN 1-60191-045-2 (Paperback)

For Mary

Table of Contents

INTRODUCTION iii
Towards an Orthodox Understanding of Pastoral Ministry: Archimandrite Kyprian Kern (1900–1960)

CHAPTER 1 1
Orthodox Pastoral Service

CHAPTER 2 13
Foundations for Pastoral Ministry

CHAPTER 3 29
Christian Pastoral Service

CHAPTER 4 37
Pastoral Calling

CHAPTER 5 47
Pastoral Frame of Mind

CHAPTER 6 65
Preparation for the Priesthood

CHAPTER 7 97
Ordination

APPENDIX 113
Two Models of the Pastorate: Levitical and Prophetic

INTRODUCTION

Towards an Orthodox Understanding of Pastoral Ministry: Archimandrite Kyprian Kern (1900–1960)

Nearly fifty years ago, the Eastern Orthodox monk and theologian, Archimandrite Kyprian Kern, explored pertinent issues regarding pastoral ministry. Kern's writings on clericalism and problems with the abuse of power and authority in the Church, for example, are as fresh today as when they were first written. Kern is probably the least known among Orthodox theologians in the West; however, his voice is now being heard for the first time in English and hopefully will inspire and encourage a new generation of clergy and laity who seek to better understand ministry in an Orthodox Christian context.

Kern's book *Orthodox Pastoral Service* (*Православное пастырское служение*) first appeared in a Russian language edition in Paris, published by the YMCA Press in 1957. This book is a collection of lecture notes from Kern's classes in pastoral ministry. Needless to say, Kern wanted this book to serve as a contribution to pastoral ministry. In this book, Kern deals with important issues such as clericalism, the importance of the Eucharist for the life of the priest, and emphasis on the intellectual, spiritual, and personal preparation for the priesthood. Finally, one could look at this book as a historical document. The reader will be surprised, for example, that very little is mentioned about the role of the laity, which seems odd since the book is about Orthodox pastoral ministry. Other contemporary colleagues of Kern, most notably Nicholas Afanasiev, Elizabeth Behr-Sigel, Mother Maria Skobtsova, and Paul Evdokimov, wrote extensively about the ministry of the laity.[1] Perhaps this omission was a simple oversight or maybe Kern was focused on preparing young men for ministry since this was his primary function as a faculty member of the St. Sergius Institute.

On the historical level, Kern has left us with a detailed exposition of pastoral ministry in 19th century Russia. The first chapter focuses primarily on several major contributions made by Russian theologians and pastors on the role and development of pastoral care, beginning largely from monastic centers and then chronicling developments up to his own mentor and teacher, Metropolitan Anthony Khrapovitsky, a

---

[1] See Michael Plekon, *Living Icons: Persons of Faith in the Eastern Church* (South Bend, IN: The University of Notre Dame Press, 2002) and also *Tradition Alive: On the Church and the Christian Life in Our Time Readings from the Eastern Church* (NY: Sheed and Ward, 2003).

bishop, scholar, and theologian, and at one time the dean of three Russian seminaries in Moscow, St. Petersburg, and Kazan.[2] The reader may find the first chapter too narrow, too historical, yet for the modern Church historian, or those interested in the development of pastoral care in the modern period, this first chapter is essential. For this reason, *Orthodox Pastoral Service* was and still is an important contribution to the development of pastoral care in the 20th century Orthodox Church. However, in order to obtain a better contextual understanding of Kern and his work, one has to look to the theological development in Russian émigré Paris. It is in the vibrant theological creativity and discussions among Russian theologians where Kern worked, lived, and wrote to which he made his own contributions.

THE PARIS SCHOOL THEOLOGIANS. From the early 1920s to the end of the 1950s, the Orthodox Christian community in Paris was reveling in a theological renaissance. For lack of a better term, scholars such as Paul Valliere and Michael Plekon have referred to this major theological movement and body of theological literature as the "Paris School."[3] The Paris School was not a thoroughly or-

---

[2] Archimandrite Kyprian Kern, "Reminiscences of Metropolitan Anthony (Khrapovitsky)," *Divine Ascent*, no. 9 (2004) pp. 107–162.

[3] Of the Paris School, the Church historian Antoine Arjak-

ganized movement but an informal gathering of like-minded people who were interested in a theological renewal and revival in the Church. Although this was not a single and identifiable school of thought, their mutual reflection on the nature of the Church, the role of the Eucharist, and the liturgical renaissance which was taking place in both the Eastern and Western Church's provided these theologians with fertile soil from which they reflected on Theology, Ecclesiology, Scripture, Liturgy, and the Church Fathers. In many ways, they continued the theological renaissance which was started in theological circles in late 19th century Russia. In his monumental work on Russian theology, Valliere points out that dating back to the mid 1800s one can see traces of a revival of Patristic, Biblical, and Dogmatic Theology, first

---

ovsky has said, "The School of Paris is a reality difficult to identify. It cannot be conceptualized. I would say that it is a movement, a symbolic reality, which the French historian Pierre Nora calls a 'place of memory,' that is, a certain relation to the Tradition of the Church ... And then again the collective memory of the Paris school is not very precise. Nobody really knows when it starts and when it finishes!" Antoine Arjakovsky in an unpublished paper delivered at St. Vladimir's Seminary 2004, "The Paris School and Eucharistic Ecclesiology in the 20th Century." See also Bishop Hilarion Alfeyev, "Theology on the Threshold of the Twentieth Century," paper delivered at the Monastery of Bose (Italy), September 15–17, 1999; Paul Valliere, *Modern Russian Theology: Bukharev, Soloviev, Bulgakov: Orthodox Theology in a New Key* (Grand Rapids, MI: William Eerdmans, 2000).

started by Archimandrite Theodore (Alexander) and then later followed by Alexei Khomyakov, Alexander Solovyov, and then introduced to the West primarily by Sergius Bulgakov and Nicholas Berdyaev among others.[4] Many of the Paris theologians were theologically trained in Russia and then immigrated West, bringing their thoughts and ideas to Paris, inspiring another generation of young people. Their combined writings continue to live and inspire people up to the present time, given the fact that their writings have resurfaced in many ways, most notably in theological conferences, articles in journals, reprints of their original writings, as well as in scholarly monographs and talks.

Likewise, many of the Paris theologians shared rich professional and personal friendships throughout the years; both Father Nicholas Afanasiev and Kyprian Kern served together on the faculty at the Saint Sergius Theological Institute in Paris in the early 1940s. Afanasiev was a prolific author whose work on ecclesiology was formative in the pre-conciliar work of Vatican II and the working document *Lumen Gentium* and whose writings are now enjoying a type of renaissance, especially with the new English translation and edition of his work *The Church of the Holy Spirit*, which will hopefully be fol-

---

[4] Alexander Schmemann, *Ultimate Questions: An Anthology of Modern Russian Religious Thought* (Crestwood, NY: St. Vladimir's Seminary Press, 1977).

lowed by *The Limits of the Church*.⁵ Afanasiev was and still remains to be an important voice within Eastern Christianity and hopefully more people will be introduced to his thought through his essays and books. His focus on the Eucharist as the sacrament of sacraments reminds us of our common vocation to offer our common prayer to God. Everything we do in Church life, meetings, projects, programs, and projects must flow from the Eucharistic table. The Eucharist cannot be reduced to what we do on Sunday morning, but we are called to live the liturgy after the liturgy during the rest of the work week, a theme to which Kern devoted himself in two major works, a large tome simply titled *Eucharist* as well as *Orthodox Pastoral Service*.

Other persons were connected in various ways; Father Sergius Bulgakov was the father confessor and spiritual advisor to Mother Maria Skobtsova and Father Alexander Schmemann and John Meyendorff were longtime friends and colleagues, first in Paris and then later at St. Vladimir's Orthodox Seminary in Crestwood, NY. Mother Maria took part in Nicolas Berdayev's Sunday evening gatherings in nearby Clamart, a type of informal philosophical salon. The list could go on. What is important is that there

---

⁵ See Nicholas Afanasiev, *The Church of the Holy Spirit*. Trans. Vitaly Permiakov, edited with an introduction by Michael Plekon (South Bend, IN: The University of Notre Dame Press, 2007).

was clearly a cross fertilization of themes, ideas, and friendships that are evident in their own lives as well as in their contributions to the life of the Church in both East and West.

In addition to the Eucharist, another major theme woven throughout their writings is the conciliar or sobornal nature of the Church. The Eastern Church is often described in terms of a "council" or what is often referred to in its Russian term as *sobornost*. The notion of conciliarity or *sobornost* stems from the understanding of the Church as being the living and vibrant body of Christ, each member having its own function yet is under the headship of Christ. It also means that humans have total freedom in Christ, to be active agents in God's saving plan, and fully alive to the world around them. Basically, this conciliarity and *sobornost* is a reflection of the Trinity. The Trinity is a unity of persons: Father, Son, and Spirit who are intimately connected to one another in a bond of love. While on the one hand they are united in love, they also maintain their individuality. Therefore, the relationship in the Church between the clergy and laity must reflect the Trinity. There is a basic equality among the people of God which begins through the sacrament of baptism; however, there is a distinction when it comes to official ministry such as we see in the three-fold office of the episcopate, presbyterate, and diaconate. The unity is best seen around the Lord's Table. When the whole people of God are united around the Lord's Supper, they offer their common prayer and worship to God through the offering of the Eucharist and then are sent back out into the world to serve others.[6]

Therefore, if both the clergy and laity are truly seeking to live according to the will of God, even among a fallen humanity with human sinfulness and arrogance, there must be an expression of love based on the example of Christ Himself. Jesus gave us the supreme example of love through His passion and crucifixion on the cross, giving up His life for others. His life was an example of loving and serving others, not using power and authority over His disciples. Thus, clergy are not called to have power and authority over the laity nor are the laity called to increase their power or authority over and against the clergy, but rather work together for the common good of all members of the Church.

According to the conciliar model, the Church maintains a hierarchical structure and order. The

---

[6] In her thorough history of the Russian Orthodox Church on the eve of the Russian Revolution, Vera Shevzov states that the term *sobornost* is closely related to the Greek terms *synaxis* and *ekklesia*, which means a "coming together" or a "meeting." Likewise the verb *sobrat*, which is related to the term *sobor*, means to gather together. Therefore, a sobornal Church is one that gathers together the entire people of God. For more information, see Vera Shevzov, *Russian Orthodoxy on the Eve of the Revolution* (New York, Oxford University Press, 2004), p. 30.

Introduction

Church is a community of baptized saints working together to build up the Body of Christ one person at a time through exercising the variety of gifts and charisms that are distributed to each by the outpouring of the Holy Spirit. This would preclude any notion of human freedom. The only power and authority in the Church is God working through the Holy Spirit in a life-giving and sustaining way. So while there is a basic equality among the people of God, there is still order and structure within the Body. The Body only exists because it is Christ's body and is held together by a continual outpouring of love which the Evangelist John so beautifully expresses when the post-resurrectional Jesus bestows the Holy Spirit upon His disciples and says, "Peace be with you. As the Father has sent Me, even so I send you" (John 20:21). Michael Plekon comments on the proper understanding of conciliarity in the following manner:

> The church is hierarchical and conciliar, neither a clerocracy not a democracy, but as the Moscow Council of 1917-18 strove to ensure, an assembly or communion of all the people of God. The bishops govern only because they have been elected to do so as the presiders at the Eucharist, namely as the servants of the servants of God. There is no division of the church into one part that rules and the other which is subject. Every Christian is by baptism prophet, priest and king... There can be as with Christ no separation, division or confusion among

those who gather around the Table. The bishops must be present to preside, along with priests and deacon and people. The pastors have no purpose without the flock to shepherd. Bishops lead because the assembly has elected them to preside and serve. All the assembly celebrates the Eucharist, hears the Gospel and seeks to enact the good news in God's world, the place of our everyday lives.[7]

The image of the Church as communion or fellowship or, in its Greek form, *koinonia*, is a powerful image, one that is always in front of us. The Church is comprised not just of individuals seeking their own interests but everyone working for the common good of all, which is best seen in the gathering around the Eucharistic table. When the entire Church body is present, the full Christ is present. We gather together and are fed with the bread of life in order to go out into the world to provide comfort, forgiveness, mercy, and love to those around us, or as the famous 4th century pastor and preacher John Chrysostom taught we must live the liturgy after the liturgy.[8] The real liturgy begins when the priest dismisses the people and they are sent back into the world to live a life of faith among others around them, family, coworkers,

---

[7] His comments are contained on the Reflections sub-page of www.ocanews.org, which was last accessed on April 25, 2006.
[8] Ion Bria, *The Liturgy after the Liturgy: Mission and Witness from an Orthodox Perspective* (NY/Geneva: WCC Press, 1996).

children, and neighbors. They return the following week to be fed and nourished once again in order to be filled with the Spirit of God. It is this robust and lively image of the Church, centered around the Eucharistic table, which is seen throughout the pages in this volume.

KYPRIAN KERN: THE EARLY YEARS. Kyprian (Constantine) Kern was born into a highly educated family, his father serving as a professor of forestry at the local university, or Lycee, in St. Petersburg, Russia. His mother, a devout Orthodox Christian, often took Constantine to the local monasteries near their family estate: Optina, Sarov, and the St. Tikhon Monastery near Kaluga. Kern received his early education at the Imperial Alexander Lycee in St. Petersburg; however, after the Lycee was closed by the acting provisional government during the wake of the Russian Revolution, Kern left for Moscow seeking to enter the Moscow Academy where he studied law. As Kern was pursuing a career in the legal profession, the All Russian Council was taking place in Moscow, and thanks to the generosity of one of his professors, he attended several of the meetings. It is noteworthy that at this same council were the young Sergius Bulgakov, Anton Kartashev, and Nicholas Berdyaev who later would be reunited together in Paris as they worked together at the St. Sergius Theological Institute.

In 1925, Kern left his Russian homeland to live in Belgrade, Serbia, and attended Belgrade University, where he eventually finished legal studies. By this time, Serbia had a formidable Russian community, many of whom had fled Russia after the Revolution. It was in Belgrade that Kern was reacquainted with Metropolitan Anthony Khrapovitsky, himself a formidable theologian serving as the director or dean of three of Russia's academies, Kazan, St. Petersburg, and Moscow. The two had met only briefly in a Moscow parish when Kern was at Moscow University. Several years later, they were reacquainted and began a longtime relationship. Khrapovitsky encouraged Kern to enter the monastic life, which he finally did several years later. Kern was one of the earliest members of the Brotherhood of St. Seraphim of Sarov a lay lead spiritual group which met frequently for prayer, mini-conferences, and to hear guest speakers. Khrapovitsky also inspired Kern to study theology, which Kern did, attending the Orthodox seminary in Bitola in southeastern Serbia; Kern wanted a rural setting, getting away from the city life of Belgrade. Later that year, Serge Bezberazov and Father Sergius Bulgakov, who were both traveling through Belgrade at that time, invited Kern to join the faculty at the new Orthodox institute in Paris. Kern was excited about this proposal, but after consulting his spiritual father and several friends, decided to continue his theological studies and remain in Serbia.

Kern would serve as Bezberazov's teaching assistant in liturgical theology.

On April 3, 1927, which was also Palm Sunday, Kern entered the monastic ranks, changing his name from Constantine to Kyprian, after the famous St. Kyprian of Serbia who lived in the 14th century. Kern was later ordained to the diaconate and to the priesthood at the Liturgy of Holy Thursday.

In 1928, a letter arrived from Metropolitan Khrapovitsky informing Kern that he was appointed to serve as the new administrator for the Russian Missionary Society in Jerusalem. The Russian Mission was started in the 18th century and had a long rich history serving as a place of prayer and pilgrimage in Palestine. Kern was only twenty eight years old and was not only a monk-priest but now an administrator for a foreign mission. Due to the importance of this post, Metropolitan Khrapovitsky elevated Kern to the rank of Archimandrite, vesting him with the mantyia and mitre. Kern lived in Jerusalem from 1928–1930, taking over the missionary work there that was started in the mid 19th century by Fr. Anthony Kapustin. Among his duties Kern was also the rector of the Monastery of the Holy Trinity in Jerusalem, which he also administered during his short tenure.

Upon returning to Serbia, Kern was once again invited to teach at St. Sergius in Paris, and this time he accepted. Kern packed up his belongings and moved to Paris, where he taught Patristics, Church History, and Liturgics. Metropolitan Evlogy (Georgevitsky), the spiritual leader of the Russian community in Western Europe, assigned Kern to be the chaplain for one of Mother Maria's houses of hospitality at rue Lourmel. However, since Mother Maria was difficult to get along with, he soon left and took up residence at St. Sergius. In addition to his teaching post, Kern also served a small Russian Orthodox community dedicated to Sts. Constantine and Helen in nearby Clamart, a suburb of Paris where the famous Russian philosopher Nicolas Berdyaev and his wife Lydia also lived and prayed.

While a professor of theology at St. Sergius, Kern was reacquainted with Sergius Bulgakov whom Kern met previously in Belgrade. Kern also worked alongside Nicholas Afanasiev, Anton Kartashev, and Georges Florovsky. Eventually, Kern and Afanasiev established the Fraternity of St. Seraphim of Sarov, an association of faculty and students who came together for prayer and fellowship. Kern also became the teacher and mentor for the young Alexander Schmemann and John Meyendorff, who later on spoke very highly of Kern's influence on them. Kern spent most of his time teaching as well as serving the small parish community in Clamart, and also during this time, he did manage to publish some theological materials, a book on the Eucharist in 1947 and then one on *Orthodox Pastoral Service* in 1957. Kern's work on the

Introduction xvii

theology of the Eucharist was also very influential on many of his students at St. Sergius, especially for the young Alexander Schmemann, who was a student under Kern and then later after his ordination to the priesthood was attached to Sts. Constantine and Helen. Kern's study and teachings on the Eucharist and on liturgical theology was so influential in the life of Alexander Schmemann that Schmemann dedicated his doctoral dissertation to Kern. In 1953, Kern together with Afanasiev established the famous "Liturgical Weeks" at St. Sergius, which gathered together clergy, laity, scholars, and theologians for a week of prayer, study, and to hear conference papers. These meetings were ecumenical and were attended by Roman Catholics, members of the Reformed Church, as well as Anglicans, and others.

In addition to his work on Patristics and Liturgy, Kern was also interested in pastoral theology and eventually wrote *Orthodox Pastoral Service*. In it, Kern traces the history of pastoral care in the Russian theological tradition from the mid-19th century to his time, highlighting particular priests and bishops who exhibited what he considered to be good pastoral ideas. This was one of the few book on the pastoral life during this time, and perhaps one of the few in France. One can see traces of Kern's thoughts on vocation and liturgy in the later work of his student Alexander Schmemann, especially in his *Journals*, where he makes glaring comments about problems with priests and confession, the incompetence of bishops, and spiritual guruism.

According to Kern, it was the Eucharistic gathering where both clergy and laity gathered around the one table of the Lord to offer their prayer and praise. He had no time for clericalism or the abuse of power and authority by the clergy over the laity, which is a theme that runs throughout his writing and which is also a theme in several of his writings, especially "Two Models of the Pastorate Levitical and Prophetic," where he shows that the prophetic priest is one who is seeking God's will in life and will risk his own stability and comfort for the preaching of the Gospel. This he contrasts with the Levitical type of the priesthood, which is best exemplified in the Old Testament image of the Temple and the Levitical priests who serve there. These priests, Kern says, exemplify a rigid formalism and ritualism which suffocates. They are too worried about rules and regulations and have no time for creativity and freedom. Kern concludes his essay by saying that these two forms of priesthoods exist today in constant tension with one another.

Kern identifies a healthy pastorate which does not identify solely with the clergy but with the entire people of God who gather around the Eucharistic table for praise and prayer. While the clergy lead the community in prayer, the entire people offer the Eucharist and where the true Church is revealed. Kern also speaks about the importance of pastoral formation, focusing primarily on the spiritual and intellectual education of clergy. While Kern lived a monastic life, he was in many ways a monk of the world, enjoying art and music, as well as what some would call secular literature. He enjoyed visiting art museums and engaging in local cultural events, always engaging in the world around him.

Vocation: Called to Serve. One of the major themes that is woven throughout *Orthodox Pastoral Service* is the importance of vocation. Looking at the historical development of the Church, Kern emphasizes that Orthodox ecclesiology is centered around the Eucharist, the sacrament of sacraments and that everything that we do is done in community, gathered around the Altar of the Lord. Likewise, one could say that we are connected to one another primarily through the sharing of a common faith in Christ expressed in our rule of prayer, especially the Lord's Prayer, Creed, the weekly celebration of the Divine Liturgy, and a common expression of love. Everything that we do cannot be of "our own" but first and foremost comes from God. We are united around the one Altar, offering our one prayer and praise to God, and receiving the one bread and cup of the Eucharist. Our primary understanding of the Church is that of *koinonia* or communion, fellowship. Everything that we do is clearly expressed in the anaphora prayers which are plural, *we* praise, *we* bless, *we* give thanks. It is our common sacrifice of praise on behalf of all and for all that we offer each and every Sunday. Therefore, to understand the concept of vocation, or calling, we have to start with the community of faith. There can be no individual calling without first the calling of the community as Kern himself says, "From time immemorial Orthodoxy has preserved the principle of electing a priest and a bishop by the people." Kern emphasizes this notion of communal calling, there is no room for radical individualism, we are all members of one another, partakers of the one bread and cup of Christ. Actually, a vocation to ministry is a three-fold process or continuum, the calling of the community of faith, the calling or invitation of the local bishop, who in his person represents the entire faith community, and then the inner calling of the individual. This three-fold calling is best expressed in the ordination service. As the candidate draws near to the Royal Doors of the Holy Altar, the people exclaim *axios*, which means worthy. The three-fold acclamation of *axios* represents the three-fold calling in the Church. However, to be called for the faith community, one must have solid theological and intellectual preparation. One of the major problems which Kern addresses and which remains today is that some ecclesiastical leaders have little theological training or preparation. The lack of training is problematic for preaching, teaching, and pastoral care, one must

Introduction

know what to say and act before entering ministry. For Kern, a young candidate for holy orders should have a thorough intellectual and spiritual preparation for ministry. After all, if one does not know the Scriptures or the Tradition, how can one adequately preach the Gospel to the world? Kern says, "As was pointed out earlier, the baby Jesus was visited not only by simple shepherds, but wise men from the East, seeking God, bearing God's highest truth beyond the world of Christianity. If, on the one hand, the Savior called simple fishermen, so on the other hand, among the people who most of all spread Christianity, was the Apostle Paul, an educated man of his time. Very early on Christianity recognized intellectuals and defenders, such as the holy martyr Justin the Philosopher, Athenagoras, Clement of Alexandria, not to mention the abundance of ecumenical teachers and pastors of the golden age of the Church." Kern fully supported a highly educated clergy, since clergy have to deal with the complexities of 20th century life, including social, political, and spiritual questions. The recent rise of Communism together with the bitter end of World War II called everything into question, "It is, therefore, quite natural that the great teachers and priests of the ecumenical Church repeatedly uttered words of warning or reproach for careless treatment of admittance to priesthood to those who sought it and to those who administered the laying of the hands."

Kern's thoughts on ministry also include spiritual preparation. Book knowledge or academic training is not separate from the "inner spiritual life" of the clergy. Faith is not only learned but also lived:

> The pastor must be kind and compassionate, which does not at all mean sentimentality, but the ability to assimilate into himself the joys, sins, sorrows and suffering of others. The pastor must be venerable, that is, becoming like Christ, who is the perfect ideal of the Good Pastor. The pastor must be prayerful, that is, loving the activity of prayer in all its manifestations, especially the private prayer, especially the Jesus Prayer, praying in Church and most of all the services of Divine Liturgy. A priest without prayer, incapable of praying, not willing to explore the elements of prayer, not attracted to liturgy and in every way, under all plausible and implausible pretexts avoiding it, is a contradiction to himself and an unproductive administrator of spirituality. The pastor must be humble, that is, devoid of a sense of pride, arrogance, conceit, ambition, vanity and egoism. Humility is not expressed by low bows before others and not at all by signing ones name with the designation of humble priest so-and-so, nor by putting self into the center of the whole world, self-admiration, etc., but in a genuine liberation from all egocentrism. The list of goals for which the priest must strive could be extended, but in the main, this is enough. All of the above may be reduced to a single condition — spirituality — that is — free-

dom from the power of any sin as well as any worldly, nationalistic and political ambitions.

AGAINST CLERICALISM. One of the first items that Kern mentions in his list of pastoral problems is ministerial ambition, which is sometimes hidden deep within a person. In the New Testament, Jesus warns us about the abuse of power and authority. Towards the end of Matthew, as Jesus approaches Jerusalem, He warns against the hypocrisy of the Pharisees and Saducees who "like their place in the synagogue and who want to be seen in the best seats and wear beautiful clothes" (Matthew 22). Jesus explicitly teaches His disciples that the Son of man did not come to be served but to serve.

Kern was fully aware of the temptations of clericalism and the abuse of power, for during his lifetime there was still much of a divide between clergy and laity, and pastors were given a lot of authority in the Church. One of his early essays, "Two Models of the Pastorate Levitical and Prophetic," which first appeared in the famous theological manifesto *Living Tradition* (*Zhivoe Predanie*) in 1937, edited by Nicolas Berdyaev, is included in the appendix of this book. This anthology was directed towards paving the way for a new push for creative and expressive theological dialogue with the Western culture, society, and religion. Kern writes at length against the overtly clerical caste system which is stagnant, uncreative, and follows the rubrics and rituals to the letter of the law. He compares this type of priesthood with that of the prophetic, which is more open to the Spirit, creative, and dynamic, "A Levitical type, in this special meaning, is one from a priestly caste, one who is conventional, formal, narrowly nationalistic, inert, and uncreative. In Old Testament times, the Mosaic Law priesthood was hereditary and exclusive."

Kern shows that the Levitical type of priest is lifeless and without spirit. We have to keep in mind that during Kern's lifetime, the clergy were members of a highly stratified caste system and functioned like local government officials. In her book *Russian Orthodoxy on the Eve of the Russian Revolution*, the Russian historian Vera Shevzov points out that the clergy not only performed the liturgical rites and rituals in the local parish but also decided low level court cases, chaired local communal meetings, and was an important figure in the local Russian village, even in the eyes of non-Orthodox members. There was a complete social and spiritual break between the ordained clergy and the common laity, the majority of whom were from the peasant class. This understanding of the clergy caste was and still is with us today as is seen in recent studies by Roman Catholic theologians on the overtly clerical state of the Catholic Church.

Kern compares the Levitical type of priest with that of the prophetic. Just as the prophet was sent by God to bring the good news to Israel, to repent and turn back to God, so too must the prophetic priest bring the good news as well. The prophets were creative, open, and not constrained to the rules and regulations of the society. Most of the prophets were thrown out of Israel and were harassed and harangued by their fellow Israelites. Kern notes that the prophetic type is rooted in freedom. God gave His people complete freedom of conscious, a theme which is also emphasized by Kern's colleagues such as Bulgakov, Berdyaev, and later his student Schmemann. Yet Kern points out that the Levitical type of pastor constricts freedom in the Church, emphasizing the rules, regulations, and rituals, while overlooking individual freedom of persons:

> The pastor must particularly keep in mind that man's moral destiny is first of all governed by freedom. Freedom always holds the dangers of evil and sin, yet in freedom there also lies goodness, which will overcome evil and sin. Christianity is God's message about freedom, which, as mentioned earlier, is quite different from propagations of revolutionary, political, and mutinous freedoms. It is a spiritual freedom. Therefore, the pastor should worry less about his inviolate authority but more about his persuasiveness about truth. The criterion of truth is in the truth itself. Compulsory authority is not characteristic of Orthodoxy. The pastor must call for acceptance of truth, for submission of self to the superior Christian freedom.

Time does not permit reviewing all the themes of this book, which is left up to the reader. We hope that Kern's voice, first heard nearly a half century ago, will now be heard again for another generation of pastors.

Needless to say, not everything in *Orthodox Pastoral Service* is of equal value. The majority of the book was comprised of lectures delivered to seminary students and, therefore, Kern includes practical advice, such as the daily schedule of the parish priest, maintaining good personal appearance and physical hygiene, what we would today consider to be general common sense. Likewise, Kern also makes several critical remarks about Roman Catholic and Reformed theology. Much of this stems from the time in which Kern lived and wrote. While, on the one hand, there was a great sense of ecumenism between various ecclesial bodies, yet, a majority of Orthodox living in the West, they wanted to preserve their distinctiveness within the Western culture and society. Therefore, the reader will find from time to time remarks which seem very strong to our modern ear, yet, for Kern, it was his way of making sense of his own theology and thought given the theological context in which he lived. One would hope that we read these negative comments in the context in which they were written.

CHAPTER 1

Orthodox Pastoral Service

The task of defining any academic discipline is far from easy, simply because the set boundaries of a given subject are not always easily defined. Every academic discipline comes into contact with other academic subjects, naturally uniting them and quite often passing the limits of their boundaries. Excessive broadening of a subject's boundaries decreases the breadth of the subject, and decreasing the boundaries narrows its meaning.

The same thing may be said regarding the limitations of a theological subject, usually called "Pastoral Theology," as will be made apparent shortly. A difficult problem arises due to the fact that not all theologians are ready to acknowledge pastoral theology as a subject; one, for example, is Professor P. I. Linitsky. It is often claimed that pastoral theology is not a subject, but merely a skill. The subject's study is not clearly defined, the study methods used are understood differently by various scholars. Thus, this science is usually relegated to the sphere of "Practical Theology," although many pastoral scholars who abandoned the sphere of "Practical Theology" are often giving it a purely theological meaning, thereby changing its character to mean "Moral Theology" or, more to the point, they give it an ascetical meaning.

One Western scholar expressed the opinion that the content, volume, and practical values of pastoral theology are unknown, merely implied, searched for but not found.[1] In any case, by defining this subject in one way or another, scholars first of all speak of pastorship, or pastoral service, or pastoral obligations. At this point, a definition must be given to pastorship itself. First of all, pastoral theology includes the study of the pastor, his activities, his responsibilities as well as his character. Therefore, the center of this subject lies in the personality and activities of the priest. However, it should be made clear that not all areas of the priest's activities enter into this realm. For example, all priestly activities dealing with Divine Liturgy are omitted from the context of pastoral theology. That subject is fully defined by liturgics. Along similar lines, the priest's work on religious instruction is studied as a separate subject, which is usually referred to as catechesis. Furthermore, the area of the pastor's preaching activities is included under the general ru-

---

[1] A. Graff, "Critical Exposition ... Substance of Pastoral Theology," Tübingen, 1841, and "Kristische Darstellung des Gegenwartigen Zustandes der Pastoraltheologie" Tübingen, 1841.

bric of homiletics. Therefore, the duties and laws that govern the priest, like those that govern judges, define the subject of canon law. By narrowing our subject, it becomes clear that pastorship deals primarily with an area outside of the pastor's worship activity. But here we are confronted with a famous contradiction: for example, the sacrament of confession presents an especially important element in pastorship. Thus, this sacrament, in its non-liturgical form, but exclusively spiritual, ascetical, morally inevitable, is included in the area of pastoral science. In any case, if not exclusive, it presents a very important subject for study by the pastoral theologian. In pastoral theology, the so-called "care of the soul" occupies a place of great importance.

The pastor is also bound by his personality. To overlook this aspect would deprive the pastoral science of its essential importance. The personality of the priest is connected to many pastoral questions, for example: pastoral calling, pastoral preparation, pastoral frame of mind, temptations during pastoral service, concerns about his family life, his behavior and so forth.

In Orthodox pastoral theology, particularly in Russia, many opinions were voiced about all these pastoral questions, giving rise to many different definitions, thereby changing the borders of pastoral science. The first pastoral theologian, Archimandrite Anthony Amfiteatrov, understood pastoral theology as a "systematic exposition of rules and instructions," leading to a successful form of pastoral service in the Christian Church and through it the Christian faith, so necessary for people's salvation; almost an identical view on pastoral theology is held by another noted Russian theologian, Metropolitan Makary Bulgakov. For Metropolitan Makary, pastoral theology is a subject which gives general instructions to the pastor in the proper conduct of his duties in leading his flock to Christian believers. These authors, in designing the courses of pastoral theology, quite often attempted to narrow its boundaries to its moral elements. For the famous award-winning theologian, Bishop Kiril Naumov, winner of Doctor of Theology degree for his "Pastoral Theology," this science represents a systematic exposition of moral obligations for the pastor of the Church.

Archimandrite Boris Plotnikov limited his explanations to moral qualities. Notably sharper and quite narrower, Archimandrite Anthony Khrapovitsky, of blessed memory, one of the greatest scholars in this area of study, defines pastoral theology, as pastoral asceticism, as a means "to direct the heart to the inner life of the pastor, consciously creating in him a pastoral feeling toward the people." Bishop Theodore Pozdeevsky, the last rector of pre-revolutionary Moscow Theological Academy, also liked to view this study as ascetical.

Archpriest A. Solerintsky, a professor of many years at the St. Petersburg Theological Academy, felt that the theme of pastoral theology should be based on the concept of Jesus Christ, the Savior. He authored a well-written book on this subject, which, however, sheds little light upon the pastoral problems that confront the priest. The exiled Protopresbyter G. Schlovetsky, the last Chief Chaplain of the Russian Imperial Army, echoed those opinions, but at the same time in his book *Orthodox Pastorship*, he tries to address a wide range of modern-day pastoral problems. An entire monograph, entitled *Pastoral Theology in Russia* by Hieromonk Innocent Pustinsky, was devoted to this subject. Reviewing the literature on the subject, the author stressed "the love of the pastor for his flock and his selflessness for the sake of the flock's interest." In this work, the strong influence of Archimandrite Khrapovitsky's lectures is quite evident.

In trying to define the boundaries of pastoral theology, the following examples come to mind: either it is limited to the moral aspects, at times even ascetical, Anthony Khrapovitsky and Theodore Posdeevsky, to a system of rules of conduct and duties of the pastor, as for example, in Palmer's "Pastoral Instructions," or it is deprived of any scientific qualities, leaving only the possibility of it being just a skill in guiding the Christian flock, not defining anything, merely speaking of "that which is sought, but not found" (Graff). In that context, pastoral theology becomes, as Hieromonk Innocent states in his preface, "not a science in the actual sense, but a complete understanding, derived from various areas of theological studies, with a definite practical aim." In any case, problematic elements cannot be excluded from the study of pastoral theology, because, in a very real sense, it is a creative part of the ever-living body of the Church. Everything does not converge only on programs, instructions, pastoral behavior, laws and duties of the pastor; this study demands answers to modern and urgent questions of pastorality, which the pastor cannot avoid facing. Therefore, it is more plausible to speak of the inherent skill of pastoral work. This does not exclude in any way the undisputed element of a higher spiritual artistry, but is presented in the form of science, much as the art of music, which also requires scientific methods, such as theory, counterpoint, harmony, and so forth. This leads to the conclusion that pastoral science speaks of: 1) the pastor, his personality, qualities, calling, preparation, attitude, *i.e.* spiritual, not just moral; 2) the very art in guiding his flock; and 3) the problems arising during the pastoral service, for example, pastoral psychoanalysis, pastoral psychology, and various other pastoral problems.

During the reign of Alexander I, before the major reforms of the theological schools, Russia had its own pastoral literature. By the end of the 18th century and at the beginning of the 19th century, there were three literary works addressing pastoral activities. The first book to be published in St. Petersburg in 1776 was entitled *The Book of Duties of the Parish Priest*. Apparently, there were two authors; Bishop Parthenius Sopkovsky of Smolensk and Archbishop George of Mogilev. Archbishop Filaret Gumilevsky regards Bishop Parthenius as its only author, although Hieromonk Innocent insists, quite convincingly, that both bishops were its authors. Although this work was quite famous in its time, it lays no claims to any study of science, but rather strives to be a summary of helpful guides for the parish priest. It has gone through many publications (twenty-one by 1833), quite a remarkable feat by the then prevailing publication standards of Russia and was even translated into English by the Rev. B. W. Blakemore.

At the beginning of the 19th century, Metropolitan Platon Levshin of Moscow published a book entitled *A Condensed Catechism* (Moscow, 1807), which was intended to serve as an introduction to the clergy and especially for those who were about to enter the Church Ministry. Judging by its title, this book was not meant to be a book of systematic study of pastoral theology but merely a practical guide. It was quite appropriate for its time and as such, along with other above-mentioned books, was translated into English.

One must not forget a third book, which does not deal directly with pastoral theology, but which nevertheless is close enough to this subject to be mentioned. It is entitled *Ortodoxae Orientalis Eclesiae Dogmate, seu Doctrina Christiana de Credentis* (part 1) *et agentis* (part 2) (Leipzig, 1874). Its author, the famous Feofilakt Gorsky, wrote it in Latin, as all theology was written and thought at that time. Essentially being the "sum total" of dogmatic and moral theology, doctrine, and practice, dealing particularly with the Mysteries and pastoral work of the priest.

The new, reformed school of theology slowly but surely realized the necessity of giving theological students a scientific guide to the study of pastoral ministry. As a result, after the abolition of the commission of Theological Institutes in 1839 and revision of programs at theological schools, two courses on pastoral theology appeared almost simultaneously. One was a book by Archbishop Anthony of Kazan (1851) and the other by Bishop Kiril (1853). The first, unfinished and quite weak in dogmatic theology, was written by an author who was a serious theologian of his time, but which suffers from many deficiencies, especially in formalism and narrowness. In the words of the historian and Professor I. Khristovich of St. Petersburg Academy, Bishop Kiril's *Pastoral Theology* was the first attempt at scientifically outlining pastoral duties and obligations.[1] It is, of course, outdated but at the same time more or less detailed and an important scientific guide.

C. Sturdza, a well-known writer of theological and Church oriented themes, is the author of useful articles about the obligations and duties of the Holy

---

[1] *History of the St. Petersburg Theological Academy*, p. 290

Orders. His articles take the practical approach to pastoral care. The same practical approach is evident in two other books: *Memorandum Book for Priests, or Reflections about Priestly Obligations* by Archbishop Platon of Kostroma (1860) and *Practical Guide for the Clergy* by P. I. Nechiev. Professor V. F. Pevnitsky was a famous Kievan pastoral theologian who wrote about pastorship and whose pastoral books, *The Priest* (Kiev, 5th edition, 1897), *Priesthood* (Kiev, 2nd edition, 1897), *The Nature of the Priest's Ministry in the Guidance of His Flock* (St. Petersburg, 3rd edition, 1898), remain valuable even today, despite its "all's well" naiveté. Those books were written for a peaceful and non-turbulent time, but they totally fail to address contemporary problems. The senior professor at St. Petersburg Theological Academy, Archpriest Solertinsky, as mentioned earlier, tried to present pastoral work as "Pastorship of the Savior." His book, which is rather dull, despite its scientific language, probably will not survive beyond its time and is unlikely to inspire anyone to spiritual qualities of skills to shepherd souls. Bishop Boris Platnikov wrote the book *Notes on Pastoral Theology*. Well educated and with a subtle understanding of many modern-day problems, Bishop Boris was held in high esteem by his colleagues and Church hierarchy, yet he was not well versed in pastorality. Not pleased with the outdated guidance of Archimandrite Anthony Amfiteatrov and Bishop Kiril Naumov, Bishop Boris went to another extreme. Instead of returning pastoral theology to the life of the Church, the spirit of the Holy Fathers and Church's traditions, he permeated it instead with Western ideology. In his book, Hieromonk Innocent compares this approach to that of Hopkin's *Pastoral Theology* (London, 1884). Thus, Bishop Boris' *Notes* is a copy, borrowed from an Anglican manual. From an Orthodox bishop and professor of pastoral theology, one would have expected a more suitable and conforming approach to the spirit of Church's study of pastoral theology.

The lectures of Archimandrite Khrapovitsky, principal of the Moscow and later Kazan Academy, were regarded as a momentous event in the history of pastoral science. Not coming from an ecclesiastical background nor bound by scholastic approaches of old manuals, yet having a great secular understanding, a vast knowledge and a gifted mind as well as a great sense of Church order, Archimandrite Anthony shed a bright light on Russian theology in general and on pastoral theology in particular. The young, twenty-eight-year old principal of the Moscow Academy brought new life to the pastoral educational system and a genuinely fresh approach to Church service. His independent mind and a vast general education were enriched by his humble disposition, loving heart, faith in the possibility of a person's transfiguration and most of all his charming simplicity. Not only students, but professors of the

Academy attended his lectures. His was a completely new approach to the subject, void of all modernizing and Western thoughts. He called his listeners to return to the spirit and tradition of the Church Fathers, building his teaching of pastoral theology upon the concept of "Suffering Love" of the pastor as well as a deep faith in the sinner's moral rebirth, founded on the teachings of the Fathers and their attitude toward the remorseful sinner. This teaching was in complete harmony with his heart and mind. There was no conflict between his pastoral teachings and his personal life. He lived the very thing he preached, fulfilling the requirements for the Doctor of Theology degree.

It is regrettable that Archimandrite Anthony neither preserved nor published his prepared lectures. His writings dealt with pastoral calling, pastoral preparation, pastoral gifts, and distinctive characteristics of Orthodox pastorality, devoid of all Western influences. Abroad, in exile, he recreated from memory parts of his lectures on the guardianship of souls. The articles from this priest comprised his short book entitled *Confession* (Warsaw, 1929). This book is invaluable for pastors during confessions and is also very useful for the laity preparing for confession.

CHAPTER 2

Foundations for Pastoral Ministry

Before studying the problems of traditional Orthodox pastorship, the main preconditions of pastorship, upon which all pastoral activities are based, must be clarified. This subject must be in full harmony with Orthodox world-view. Pastorship presupposes these known conditions. To be a pastor in isolation. A secluded life is a special form of service to God, but it excludes the essential elements, which flow from pastoral work. The pastor functions in the world, among people; therefore, it is important to know what type of relationship the future pastor will bring to the world and to society. It is imperative to determine this man's relationship to the world. The pastor must have a correct understanding of the world and its society, a society which, with its heavy weight upon the pastor, pulls him down to earth and away from God. Therefore, the first question that confronts us is: "What is the World?"

It must be immediately admitted that this term, as used in theological literature, is often ambiguous.

The world, aside from its literal sense, is often used in theological writings in an ascetical way. We shall turn to the second meaning of this word, "World," as it is used in its spiritually moral category, and explore its literal sense later.

The term world, used as an expression of our asceticism, denotes a certain condition of our souls. This is not an exterior expression of humanity, but rather an inner personal condition. This theme is taught in the Holy Scriptures and in all of patristic literature. The world, in the Christian sense, is clearly expressed in the Johannine writings, "The whole world lies under the sway of the wicked one" (1 John 5:19); "He was of the world and the world was made through Him, and the world did not know Him" (John 1:17). To this the Apostle Paul adds: "In the wisdom of God, the world through wisdom did not know God" (1 Corinthians: 1:21). Furthermore: "The world hated God and Christ" (John 7:7, 15: 18–19). Thus, the pessimistic outlook on the world is understandable, "And the world is passing away, and the lust of it; but he who does the will of God abides forever" (1 John 2:17). An Old Testament verse comes to mind: "Vanity of vanities and all is vanity" (Eccles. 1:2).

By examining patristic writings, it becomes quite clear that the world represents complete hostility toward God and the powers of good that are directed toward man. The whole world lies in sin. It is completely infected and poisoned by sin. But an easy and quick exit is not possible. Yet sin is only the shell of the world. Evil does not exist in the essence or nature of the world, merely in what surrounds it and envelops it. The world is not in itself evil, but lies in evil. Quoted here are various passages purposely selected from the writings of the most ascetical Holy Fathers, who seemed to be predisposed to a strict and uncompromising outlook toward creation. Saint Isaac the Syrian writes: "'World' is a collective word, encompassing within itself our countless passions. The World is carnal living and carnal wisdom." Abba Isaiah of Nitra teaches: "World — it is the habitat of sin. It is an unnatural sphere. It is the fulfillment of carnal desires. It is the idea that one will always exist in this world. 'World' personifies the care of one's body above one's soul. 'World' means worrying about things that someday will be left behind..." "Love of God," St. Mark the Ascetic adds to this the following: "Because of our passions, we were given the commandment not to love the world, nor that which is of the world. This does not mean that we should thoughtlessly hate God's creation, but rather cut ourselves off from all worldly passions." Theoleptus of Philadelphia used this expression: "I call the love of flesh and all things material worldly."

It becomes clear from these writings that "world," in the language of Orthodox asceticism, does not denote the empirical world, nature or God's creation, but a certain negative spirituality. Creation, as such, is not at fault. There is a literary profusion of stories about ascetics who loved God's creation, animals and all of nature. Orthodox ascetics embrace God's creation with joy, love and respect.

This reverence and respect requires a substantial change in the usage of this word. "World" does not only represent the sum total of passions or sins, but above all the reality of God's creation. It must be remembered that all creation is "good." The created world is but a reflection of the uncreated Godly plan upon which the Creator founded our surrounding cosmos. For all its richness and glory, there is only one word in the Greek language — cosmos — to describe "world" and "beauty." Creation, even if fallen, is of divine origin. It was already in existence in God's divine plan for the world. This event, this Godly structure of the world is the reflection of a different reality, not empirical, which gives rich material for the "symbolic realism" of the Holy Fathers and abundant means for deeper contemplation of the world as well as our selves. Only through divine origin can creation be blessed and undergo transfiguration. If the world itself is evil, this would mean that it was created evil. But evil, as taught by St. Maximus the Confessor, is not the natural essence of creation, but its foolish and sinful usage.

It is necessary to draw forth clear and logical conclusions when dealing with Orthodox dogmatic theology. It is time to stop questioning what God does not question, proclaiming what God does not proclaim. Christianity defeated Monophysitism, but as a Western historian correctly pointed out, it did not overcome the famous "psychological monophysitism." This "psychological monophysitism," this human and worldly aversion to acknowledge God's creation, throws a thin, yet strong cloud over asceticism, literature, liturgy and ethics of Christianity. The pastor must understand this and firmly oppose it. One must always bear in mind the resolution of the Gangra Council, condemning excessive asceticism and pseudo-pious Puritanism which have no place in the strict Orthodox world-view; this, then, must be the cosmological basis of pastorship.

Some beautiful thoughts of contemporary writers and ecclesiastics serve as examples to help clarify the statements made by the Holy Fathers. For instance, the French Catholic philosopher Jacques Maritain,[1] wittingly points out the three main heresies in viewing the world:

1. "Satanic Division" considers the world evil, doomed and not subject to the transfiguring light of Christianity. Easily succumbing to this outlook are the doctrines of reformation, especially Barthianism, our sectarianism, old ritualism and nihilism.

2. "Theocratic" heresy considers that the world can become God's kingdom and that this latter event may be accomplished within the boundaries of this

---

[1] *Humanisme intégral*, pp. 113–118

historical epoch. This is the heresy about the temptation of Byzantium and is perhaps a part of the Russian Church.

3. "Anthropocentric Humanism" typifies the philosophy of the august Kant. It is a reverse approach, for here is the direct "secularization" of the Kingdom of God. The world is, and can only be, the domain of man. God must be banished from it. Put another way, this is the Utopia of pure humanism.

In acknowledging the various above-stated opinions about the world, as well as by realizing the grave dangers of judging the "world and all that is in it" so superficially, it is appropriate to bring out excerpted observations from the travel diary of Archimandrite Antonin Kapustin, a pilgrim, in the mid-eighteenth century, who was on his way to Mount Athos, "The constant complaining of the monks about the world are neither clear nor logical. For the monks of the Holy Mountain, the world begins at the monastery's threshold, for the recluse — the cell is the world, for the hermit — the world is everything that lies beyond his cave or wilderness. What then is "World"? "World" is the society of man. But the society of man is man himself. Where can one escape from one's self?

Countess Catherine Efimovskaya, Mother Superior, founder and prioress of the celebrated Lesninky Monastery, who loved literature, life and people, was fond of saying: "It is not only necessary to save one's self from the world, but to save the world as well." In order to clarify the ideological basis of pastorship, a second question begs to be answered. The pastor-priest has to know what his relationship will be toward man. Just as in the first question, the anthropological premise of pastorship anticipates great difficulties. The greater danger here, more than in the previous case, lies in the temptation of solving problems in a simplistic manner.

Anthropology is the science of man, which in the philosophical sense often takes a biological form, since quite naturally science is seen from man's naturalistic point of view, as principally a common combination of cells, tissues, nerves and a mass of various psychological processes. "Science," according to Nesmelov, "views man only as food for worms." On the other hand, for the theologian and the philosopher, it is more appropriate to view man not as a science, but as an enigma; the Delphinian expression "know thyself" has an eternal meaning and application. To explain this meaning logically and rationally is often impossible. It is very easy to get embroiled in man's hostile existence, and it is dangerous and naïve to pass a hasty judgment over man's various actions.

Man belongs to two worlds on both planes of existence: spiritual and physical. He is not merely a simple thing of the physical world to which he belongs bodily, with all its complex systematic psychological processes, of which we have spoken. Man's spirit and personality reject this world and refuse to be subordinated to its binding and coercive, implacable laws.

Its narrow determining frames suffocate him as he strives to break out of them. He protests against these laws of nature with his freedom, his personality and his thirst for creativity. Man is a contradiction between upholding the present way of life and its ideal applications. In acknowledgment of these contradictions lies the mystery of man. This goal, which every man sets for his life, cannot be easily and optimistically accomplished. Living in the reality of this world, man is faced with the inevitable knowledge that accomplishing this goal is not possible.

The ideal, the spiritual side of man is of much greater interest to the philosopher, theologian and priest, and therein are to be found the central unsolvable problems which constitute the mystery of man. We will present some of the most important ones.

1. Personality: On this subject, the Christian religion provides the most complete revelation of man's unique beginning, distinguishable from any other type of being. The ancient pagan world had no concept of personality. Although the Hellenistic mind rose to the utmost heights (of that era's) philosophical awareness, with keen debates swirling around the Trinitarian and Christian dogmas, it was not able to define "personality." Christianity was the divine basis of personality. Trinitarian debates imparted the theological foundation to man's personality by acknowledging the Person and Hypostasis in God. The Greek language with its highly sophisticated philosophical

minds — Plato and Plotinus — was content with the pronoun "ekastos" or "every" describing it with the article "the ekastos," characterizing it as "member" and ascribing to it a strict individuality. Yet, it still remained merely a pronoun, rather than a "noun." Only the theological understanding of "Hypostasis," premise of independent existence, enabled it to fill the void in the language, which, in the contemporary dictionary is known as "Personality." A person is not a mere individual, a part of an appearance, a result of the biological birth process, something mortal, as some number in a naturalistic order, not whole, fully repetitive. Personality is the imprint of the Divine Person, God's creation, not merely the issue of the human race. Personality is divine and belongs, above all, to the divine world. This is the supreme value of divine existence.

Add to all these different definitions between individualism and personality, as it is clearly defined by the philosophy of Berdyaev, his remarks that "man is not a separate part of the world, for within him lies the enigma and the solution to the enigma of the world."[1] Man's personality is not the product of society, nor his innate world, not even his race or family. Spiritually, each person is God's direct creation. Man is not dependent upon the origin of birth, race or the world. Man's spirit is higher and wider, above race, society

---

[1] *About Man's Purpose*, p. 50

and the world. Community did not bestow this spirit upon man; therefore, it is not part of mankind. Man either embraces and welcomes it or rejects it. The human race and society consist of man's individuality, but man's spirit and personality are not a part of the human race or society. Man's spirit may depend on the human race and society as much as he likes, but in no case is he a part of them or a slave to them. Personality is above society and far more important. Besides, no one's personality can be replicated and cannot be replaced with "the same kind" of personality. "The same kind" of personality does not exist. The same impressions, imprints, serial numbers, as produced by a machine, exist, but each personality, no matter how many millions upon millions the historical process has produced, remains unique.

2. Freedom — Man's divine origin is reflected in his very being. There is a spark of God's freedom in man. As much as man belongs to other areas of existence, consisting in part of various aspects, such as race, birth, family, society, social standing, pack mentality, as for example: submission, whether willingly or unwillingly, to the laws of nature, by which these groups are formed and by which they live (*i.e.* monasticism), he is free to decide to rise up against these natural laws or submit to these laws more or less without controversy. By virtue of his divine origin and divine spark of freedom, man is able to reject these natural laws. Man can refuse to keep in step with

humanity and society and oppose it, unlike bees, ants or other creatures. Above all else, when speaking of human freedom, it must be clearly remembered that theology does not refer to political freedom, as advocated by national platforms and by "stormy" impulses of rebellious youth. Human freedom, which can be of interest only to a reasonable, thinking, theological human being, is spiritual freedom. Its goal is not political independence but freedom of the human spirit from all that lowers and deprives it of its divine nature. This freedom is not arbitrary, as is the dream of the anarchists and rebels; it is not stubbornness, but the release of one's spirit from what can fundamentally lower spiritual values and substitute in its place other, non-spiritual ones. This freedom does not subordinate itself to the force of evil, sin or other worldly non-spiritual values, but frees man from the absolute power of mankind and society over his religious independence. The acceptance of this freedom is perhaps deeply embedded in man's consciousness, yet it still remains paradoxical.

A — First of all, man, according to the remarks of Nesmelov, may utterly misunderstand the concept of freedom, for this understanding involves a fairly complex process of development of thoughts; however, not to possess this consciousness is impossible, for, in fact, man acts only in the name of this consciousness.

B — It does not matter how unconditionally and how above all else man accepts this freedom (human feelings, family, society and etc.). Freedom is a compulsory gift. At birth, man does not ask if he wants to be born (spiritually) free, a slave or as a part of a group. Our freedom is given to us without our free consent. This is, perhaps, the greatest paradox of freedom.

C — Freedom, no matter how much all who wish to acquire it, day-dream about it, at some time or another realize that freedom is always tied to responsibility, and as a result of that, lightly reject it. Dostoyevsky understood this. They who probe into the human soul, who strive to shepherd the human soul through "dictatorship of conscience," know it also. This could easily be called "paternalistic" in spite of the fact that it has nothing in common with real paternalism. The priest has to know and must remember this.

The moral virtue of man presents one of the problems of Christian anthropology. It cannot undergo simplifications, no matter how tempting those simplifications may be many. Humanity's strivings for purity and holiness are firmly embedded in the image and likeness of God, yet all of life's experiences teach the impossibility of reaching this ideal. There is a longing in mankind for our heavenly home, longing for the lost paradise, yet at the same time there is a heavy load, a great weight dragging us down. No one could express it better than the Apostle Paul in chapter seven in his instructions to the Romans about the two laws — the law of the mind and the law of the flesh; his words constantly conveying in his reproach to the essential experiences of life, not only his, but mankind's, in aspiring to fulfill the law of the mind: "For the good that I will to do, I do not do, but the evil I will not to do, that I practice" (Romans 7:19).

Christian asceticism aspires to realize the ideal purity of the mind and strives to overcome the hostility of the two laws. Yet, there are dangerous rocks submerged underwater for the layman, monk, priest and their guides. Asceticism does not dare to be mixed up with negativity. If monasticism is to be acknowledged as the highest moral aspiration of the Christian spirit, which does not at all mean that monks are always the ideal Christians, it chooses to protect itself with three known ordinances: poverty, obedience and abstinence. This means: not to own material things, not to marry and in general not to give in to delights of the flesh and not to exercise one's own will. But these three negations cannot be considered the ideals of Christian spiritual activity, because they require a non-active participation. This refers only to the first part of the Psalm's verse "Deviate from evil," but it pays no attention to the second verse: "and do good." Man has been called to do good, but this good does not consist of creating moral values only. Man is commanded to be a creator, as befits the image of his Creator. Therefore, this man-creator must, here on earth, obey his Creator and produce all kinds of good in the realm of moral virtue as well as in the world of spirituality, intellect, in the arts, and in science. This is precisely how the biblical words: "in the image and likeness" were viewed by the most thoughtful theologians and writers of old, such as St. Gregory of Nyssa, the blessed Theodoritus, Basil of Seleucia, St. Anastasius the Sinaite, St. Photius of Constantinople, St. John of Damascus, and St. Gregory Palamas.

Man must create good, not merely abstain from evil. In his activities, man rises above the common imitations. By being aware of this power to create, the pastor must be especially wise and thoughtful, for here are the richest educational means of pastoral nourishing of souls.

Perhaps man's creative instinct serves him as a weapon in the fight against many temptations. Man may use his inborn powers of creativity for sinfulness, which in turn will lead him to unfaithfulness. Yet, these same creative forces may prove to be his means of salvation by transforming his evil instincts, which are directed at his base impulses. The precise term, well known to modern psychoanalysis, is the sublimation of our dormant powers. The pastor can at this point awaken in the man-slave to passions and vices, the spirit of the creator and artist and save him from boredom and hopelessness.

Without further expanding upon any additional questions, it may be said that the mystery of man, about which so profoundly wrote the Orthodox thinker Nesmelov, the Catholic psychologist John Klug and the Protestant theologian Emil Brunner, dares not limit the pastor to only moral categories of good and evil, holiness and sin, since this mystery quite often oversteps into the realm of suffering and tragedy, conflicts and hostility. In antiquity, Plotinus said: "In truth, man is not a harmony." This, before all else, the pastor who wishes to shepherd his flock wisely and save it from all modern dangers and paradoxes, must always remember. Man cannot be stylized as a sinner or a righteous being, for there is an abundance of each to be found in this mysterious hieroglyph that steps beyond the limits of moral theology and which requires a thoughtful and moral Christian psychoanalysis.

CHAPTER 3

Christian Pastoral Service

The preceding chapter dealt with the ideological foundation of pastoral ministry. Let us briefly review the foundations for pastoral ministry, which do not come from nothing, but flow in the world and among people. The world is the sum total of hostility toward God and goodness; it is a domain that lies in evil, yet the world, like the empirical creation, is not itself evil. Man, even if fallen, is still the image of God: "I am the image of Thy ineffable glory, even as I bear the ulcer of transgressions." There may be a whirlpool of sin in the depths of man's soul, nevertheless man remains God's loved being, whom the pastor cannot help but love, as he cannot help but love the world — the empirical creation.

Pastoral actions and passions, which some pastors philosophically compare to salvation, are the results of man's inner consciousness of the Kingdom of God. This consciousness of Christ's kingdom, this new creation of Christ, is, of course, a battle against the kingdom of evil, evil that is present in all of us. But goodness and evil cannot be understood without, as previously mentioned, a free will. Goodness, to which the pastor summons us, is only goodness freely accepted. Forced goodness is no longer goodness. Goodness is only goodness when it is not distorted by evil, force, compulsion or threats of terrible torments.

These, then, are the ideological preconditions of pastoral service. They require a most thoughtful maintenance of the pastor's own inner attitude. Viewing this subject in a historical setting, it becomes clear that the quality of Orthodox Christian pastoral counseling differs from other types of non-Christian services.

There exists a predominant type of sacred priesthood in paganism. The priest, shaman or sorcerer appears to be the chief mediator between man and what he calls the Divine. He offers sacrifices; he exorcizes, mollifies the angered God; he casts spells to cure human ills and guards man against evil fate. The highest point of pagan religious consciousness is reached when man rises above the primitive level of religious experiences and awakens to mystical religious feelings. At this point, an even stronger belief in the leadership of the pagan priest in the sphere of mysticism manifests itself, a sphere other religious authorities cannot attain. Mystic, sorcerer, diviner, the priest could fathom the secret worlds, worlds that were not open to the common man and the ordinary pagan. At the height of pre-Christian religious consciousness, a yearning for a genuine spirituality emerged, a yearning, which could not be fulfilled by the then popular religious culture. Exorcism and esoteric rituals were typical in paganism. In the mystical cults of priesthood and its ordination, the coming of authentic revelations were keenly and deeply felt and thirsted for. But even for the pagan priest, the requirements for spiritual leadership are rather significant.

The Old Testament presents a considerably higher understanding of pastoral ministry. The cultivation of the priestly code, especially in the post-captivity period of Israel's history, in the majority of cases stood side by side and was tied to other responsibilities, unknown in paganism, responsibilities which represented only a partial characteristic of its priestly class. By far, a greater cultivation of ethical norms is inherent in the Old Testament. Even before Christ, the most perfect moral code was well known to the priest. The Old Testament developed an understanding of holiness, absent from other religions of the ancient world. The biblical religious ideal gave a definite understanding to righteousness, expressing itself in the fulfillment of the instructions of the law. These laws, these norms were predominant in the old biblical consciousness. They were elevated above any other ancient ethical conceptions, yet they carried within themselves their own weakness. The law, the sum total of the commandments, had to be fulfilled for justification, yet did not itself give the power for fulfillment of these commandments. Above all, the law left man hopeless, constantly pointing out to him his weaknesses, imperfections and iniquities. "Weakness of the Law" is the theme of Pauline apostolic writings. Weakness of man could not be filled by the weakness of the law. Man remained, in the face of the ideally righteous law, just as remote from God as an unrighteous one. The law did not empower the sanctification of man's spirit and did not impart the means for attaining that holiness to which it so clearly pointed.

The law taught goodness, yet at the same time exposed man's lack of goodness, leaving him hopelessly seeking this goodness and exhausted under the burden of regulations of this law. Israel knew no compassion for the sinner. The Prophet Elijah, who zealously and with complete fervor was seeking God, hated not only sin, but also the sinner. He is merciless to man and creature; he command the elements, even death, yet feels no mercy for the fallen.

The Old Testament priesthood was powerless before God and could not bring comfort to the sinful man. The rabbinical directions concerning the impurity of man and animals in many situations of life gave rise to a detailed code of various oblations, sacrifices, burnt offerings, all of which failed to bring man nearer to God or God nearer to man. The strict understanding of selectivity and circumcision, as a sign of a covenant with God resulted in alienation from other people. In the sphere of the Old Testament's moral and religious concepts, it is the priest who performs the religious rites. All of Israel is considered God's sons and people, yet the understanding about the adoption of man as God's creation did not exist in the ancient religious ideas.

Only the good news of the New Testament brought new revelations about the priesthood and real pastoral ministry. The gospel of Jesus Christ taught anew about our adoption as sons and heirs; every man is the Son of God and may call God "Father." The apostolic preaching gave man hope to be in communion with God. These sermons were later expanded upon by the theology of Sts. Athanasius, Gregory the Theologian, Gregory Nazianzus, Maximus the Confessor, Symeon the New Theologian and Gregory Palamas, developing into the final study of deification, the beginnings of which reach back to Plato and Plotinus. The Gospels gave mankind faith that in Christ, we are a new creation. The transformation of humanity into the image of God and the ascent of our essence to be above the established angelic order inspire man in his Christian self-awareness. Christian humanism, as opposed to pagan and revolutionary humanism, engenders man's understanding of self. In Christ, all the limits and confines that were insurmountable for pagans and Jews have been overcome. In the realm of the Gospel, "There is neither Jew nor Greek, There is neither slave nor free, there is neither male or female, for you are all one in Christ Jesus" (Galatians 3:26–28). Christianity brings glad tidings, a full acceptance of the world, creation, nature and, of course, man, the best creation, created in the image of the Creator.

Because of this, the substance and quality of the Christian priesthood and pastoral ministry are quite different from the pagan and Jewish Levitical priesthood. The Christian priest is the builder of Mysteries, builder of the Body of Christ. He is called, and through him others also, to build a new blessed Kingdom. The Christian priest is called upon to propagate man's adoption by God; to gather all the dispersed children of God into the transfiguration of the world and mankind. Obviously, neither the moral perfection of the Gospels nor the cultivation of dogmatic truths are the most important elements of Christianity. The most important element — that is God incarnate Himself, "Great is the mystery of Godliness" (1 Timothy 3:16). The mystery of God's humanity underlies the very foundation of Christian propagation, our Eucharistic life, our ascetic spirituality. God is not only man's and the world's primary reason of life, but also its final goal. "God's Material" process, mentioned in the writings of Vladimir Solovyov, is the propagation of worldwide perfection, which only He dared to teach, Who is the Creator. This predetermines the relationship of the Christian pastor to the world and to man. This subject was discussed in the previous chapter.

Man, in whose society the priest is called to serve, was, is, and will always be, in spite of all his sins and degradations, God's beloved creation. For this reason, the Orthodox priest must be inspired by faith in man, his predestination in the everlasting assembly, communication with God Incarnate, his kin in the flesh, according to the words of Symeon the New Theologian. To that end, the priest's most important means of communication must be based upon the Good News of salvation, universal faith in this salvation and worship, instead of upon the premise of the promise of fire and brimstone.

Characteristically, pastoral counseling should strive to overcome the evil in the world and in man with goodness and love rather than with accusations and condemnations. He must be more concerned with salvation than with anticipation of Judgment Day and condemnations of all heretics, sinners, and dissidents. He must remember, based on the history of all the saints, that a complete righteous man and a complete sinner do not exist. From the heights of holiness, degradation can occur, yet repentance and rebirth are possible even from those depths of degenerations that seem hopeless. The pastor must particularly keep in mind that man's moral destiny is first of all governed by freedom. Freedom always holds the dangers of evil and sin, yet in freedom there also lies goodness, which will overcome evil and sin. Christianity is God's message about freedom, which, as mentioned earlier, is quite different from propagations of revolutionary, political and mutinous freedoms. It is a spiritual freedom. Therefore, the pastor should worry less about his personal authority but more about his persuasiveness about the truth. The criterion of truth is in the truth itself. Compulsory authority is not characteristic of Orthodoxy. The pastor must call for acceptance of truth, for submission of self to the superior Christian freedom. In his "Admonitions to Chastity," Evagrius says: "God created heaven and earth. There is no angel who could not sin and not a demon who is evil by nature. God has created the one and the other and gave both a free will."[1]

---

[1] *Love of Goodness*, volume 1, chapter 645

CHAPTER 4

Pastoral Calling

In all courses in pastoral theology, the question of pastoral calling is usually given sufficient attention, yet not all pastoral theologians approach this subject equally. It is perfectly clear that a calling to any service represents a significant promise to accomplish the task at hand. The love for the calling or service, which man undertakes freely, determines his attitude toward it. To perform any service under coercion and without prior affinity predetermines its fate to infertility and death. At his ordination, the priest is presented with a particularly mysterious gift, or "pledge, for which he will be held accountable until the 'Day of the Final Judgment'" (words after he has received a particle of the Holy Lamb). In the Holy Scriptures of both testaments, a good deal is said about vocation. The services of the prophets were particularly dependent upon the calling from on high. This service does not arise from a willful rapture, but is given to those especially called by the Superior Heavenly Pastor and not for anyone selected at random. The calling voice to this particular service is clearly heard. The emphasis, however, should focus on the question about the person who was made aware of this call, yet did not respond to its demands. Can everything that seems to be a calling, in effect be a true calling?

The words in the Old Testament make the pre-ordination of His chosen to prophetic service quite clear: "'Before I formed you in the womb, I knew you, and before you were born, I consecrated you. I appointed you a prophet to the nations.' Then I said: 'Ah, Lord God, I do not know how to speak, for I am only a youth.' But the Lord said to me: 'Do not say 'I am only a youth,' for to all to whom I send you, you shall go, and whatever I command you to say, you shall speak" (Jeremiah 1:4–7). "God also called Abraham, and blessed him and made him many" (Isaiah 51:2). The Apostle Paul also speaks in his epistle to the Romans (chapter 4) and the Hebrews (chapter 11). From the masses that followed Him, the Lord chose twelve disciples; the Holy Spirit orders: "Now separate to Me Barnabas and Saul for the work to which I have called them" (Acts 13:2). This Saul, later becoming Paul, spoke bravely about his own holy calling, "Who has saved us and called us with a holy calling, not according to our works, but according to His own purpose and grace, which was given to us in Christ Jesus before time began" (2 Timothy 1:9). His epistles are signed: "Paul, called to be an apostle..." (Romans

1:1; 1 Corinthians 1), or even, "Paul, an apostle, not from man or through man, but through Jesus Christ and God the Father, who raised Him from the dead" (Galatians: 1:1).

Also of special interest is the Apostle Paul's first epistle to Timothy: "The saying is sure: if any man aspires to the office of bishop, he desires a noble task" (1 Timothy 3:1). In translation, these apostolic words sound much more insignificant than in the original Greek. In Russian, both words "aspire" and "desire" are translated as "desire." In Church Slavonic, this is translated in the first instance as "wishes" and in the second instance "desire," which are essentially almost interchangeable. There is no distinction made in the Serbian translation between the two verbs: "want" and "desire," nor does a difference exist in the French or Latin translations. In both cases, the same verb, *desirat*, is used. The French version does differentiate to a small degree between the two verbs, yet does not strongly convey the original and special concept: *Si quelqu'un aspire à être évêque, il désire une charge excellente*. The English and German versions also do not differentiate, keeping in both translations the verb "desire" and *begehren*. The original Greek language does not only utilize two different verbs, but conveys in one as well as in the other instance a much stronger and more vivid meaning, "If one aspires to the office of bishop," the Greek version means literally as, "having a taste for the episcopate," "having an appetite for the episcopate." With these expressions, the Apostle Paul stresses not merely a desire for prelacy, a priestly service, but a sense of appetite for this service, while in the second instance, he speaks not of a simple striving, but of a strong striving, of "lust." At this point, it is assumed that the candidate possesses a particular propensity for this service, not just a mere desire. This predisposition may be assumed to be a sense of calling for the given task, which is how Bishop Theophan the Recluse interprets this subject.

In the study of pastoral service, the question of calling is understood in different ways. Roman Catholics, in their characteristic eagerness, seek to clarify, parse and classify everything according to reason. They teach about an inner calling (*vocatis interna*), as well as an external calling (*vocatio externa*). The former term identifies a kind of inner aspiration, a desire of the soul, an inner voice, calling man to a different life, away from the usual worldly one. The latter term, the call of the "external," is in all probability some outside push, a meeting of some clergyman, resulting in the transformation of the person's whole life, or some illness, upheaval, loss of a loved one: all of which can suddenly change one's outlook on life; among the many examples are: Anthony the Great, Ephraim the Syrian, Francis of Assisi, Ignatius Loyola, and many others in the history of selfless pastoral devotion.

Russian pastoral theological study takes a different approach. Bishop Boris, for one, takes a thoughtful and critical theological approach to this subject, by no means, however, denying the necessity of a calling for pastoral service. Others simplified the problems, as, for example, Archbishop Anthony Amfiteatrov of Kazan, who perceived the calling purely external and one may say, an incidental fact:

> A. Spiritual calling originating in instructions at a spiritual school.
>
> B. Education in subjects taught at all theological schools and a proper appraisal of one's abilities, successes and behavior.
>
> C. Inner disposition and love of the priesthood.
>
> D. Becoming a priest at the pleasure of the local bishop.

Archimandrite Anthony Khrapovitsky, subsequently Metropolitan of Kiev, expresses a harsher, more explicit view on the above subject. He simply and categorically denies the very possibility of a calling. He regards the sensation of God's voice in one's heart nothing more than the result of self-deception, "Catholic theologians assert that every priesthood candidate must hear this voice, but we believe that this voice can be heard only by those candidates who are instructed by the Church. Self-appraisal, self-evaluation for those preparing for priesthood are of no importance. Therefore, all discussions of pastoral calling are to be dismissed by our leading pastorate and replaced with the teaching of pastoral preparation" (*Lectures*). The question of this preparation is to no small extent initiated and covered in theological courses, yet it does not replace the very fact of the inner voice, which is sensed by some and is completely absent in others. Of course, self-deception is always possible, and an inner restraint is especially necessary in any discussions of the "spirit," but here Metropolitan Anthony differs: he completely denies any mystical feelings in a person's spiritual life. Metropolitan Anthony's extreme denial regarding all mysticism, even the very word "mysticism," regardless of its frequent usage by such writers as Maximus the Confessor and others, was completely beside the point to him. Theologically, he was an extreme rationalist and minimalist.

On the one hand, there are denials of the spiritual voice and, on the other hand, it is impossible not to acknowledge the highly indefinite "controlling power of the Church." What now? How would originating in a family of a clergyman or compulsory enrollment of a youth in a seminary, a youth who has no understanding whatsoever of the priesthood, and generally speaking, of anything else for that matter, or the very unfortunate symptom — a scholarship at a religious school, a scholarship which other schools do not offer, affect one's place in pre-revolutionary Russia? Until the upheaval of 1945, similar conditions were also prevalent in the Serbian Church. Besides, one must

Pastoral Calling

not forget the fact of the massive flight of seminarians and Academy students, caught there by their social standing, who later filled the ranks of excise departments or state house workers. The same Metropolitan Anthony in turn called these former seminarians "Rakitins" (or brooms — à la Dostoyevsky). To wit, the "Rakitins," for lack of purpose, were considered to be the school's renegades.

So to what exactly could we attribute the valid signs of a calling or a non-calling? And generally speaking, do such objective traits as a person's calling for priestly service really exist? The military service quite naturally requires manly courage, bravery and militancy; the artistic activities require a feeling for beauty, refinement of the soul and so on; therefore, what sign does one have to possess, he who considers himself to be called, to perform pastoral service and, conversely, will the absence of such a sign be sufficient for a "non-called" candidate? Here then, roughly, is what must be considered an absolute sign of a non-calling:

>1 — Seeking the priesthood for materialistic gains.
>
>2 — Political or national considerations; in other words, preparing oneself for the priesthood for the "salvation of Russia," for the restoration of "Holy Russia," as well as one or the other political system in one's homeland, or

for the sake of implementing a known national propaganda which happens to be convenient and convincing. The Church and the priesthood have more important problems to solve than these national and political impulses, no matter what their colors may be.

3 — Ambitious motives. A desire for a ruling position, a wish to make a career out of the priesthood, to become a member of a higher order, to be a leader of the people, society, or to belong to a well-known and respected order of society.

4 — Aesthetical motives. A young man's attraction to the beauty of the Divine Liturgy, the singing of hymns, the splendor of the rituals and so on and so forth. Such enthusiasm quickly vanishes, leaving only but dust in their wake. This sort of a "calling" soon becomes simply a passing emotion.

5 — As pointed out earlier, the very fact of enrollment in a theological school or belonging to a theological social class represents a purely formalistic sign and in no way signifies a genuine calling.

6 — It must not be taken as the heart's calling if the causes are: aversion to life, disappointment and antipathy for all things that earlier delighted. This state of mind and fervor are clearly fleeting. Disillusionment

about one thing cannot serve as a sign of calling for something else. L. Blue had put it exceptionally well when he stated: "There is one romantic foolishness, the thought that antipathy, aversion to life is a sign of a religious calling." God requires not an exhausted soul, nor a disenchanted and weakened spirit, but a heart full of enthusiasm, heroism, sacrifice, constructive impulses in the very holy service of the building of the Body of Christ.

Here, then, are signs that a person has been called, or, according to the words of the Apostle, has a taste for pastoral service:

1 — First of all, there ought to be a free inclination to the great and holy priestly service.

2 — A desire to create the Kingdom of God, the Body of Christ, rather than an earthly realm, its undertone notwithstanding.

3 — Readiness for sacrificial service to one's neighbors and a perception of pastoral service as a yoke of Christ.

4 — Readiness to exhibit compassion for the sinful and the sick, the sorrowful man.

5 — Readiness for persecution at the hands of the world and its principalities, a fearless denial of all conformity to the world.

6 — Consciousness of one's unworthiness and a striving for a Christ-like humility,

rather than denunciation, condemnation and disparagement of non-conformists.

7 — To experience faith, live a scriptural life, and submit oneself to the worshipful service of God.

CHAPTER 5

Pastoral Frame of Mind

This subject represents the cornerstone of pastoral service, it shapes the pivotal, innermost capacity of a priest. Here one must not speak so much about content, but more about the direction of the priest's heart. The extent of study or other priestly understanding, that is, preparations, for pastoral service will be dealt with in the next chapter. Here the immediate question to be discussed is the direction of the spiritual perception of the pastor, or, putting it another way, what distinguishes pastoral services from all other services of the Church?

This subject is viewed in various forms. For a long time, in the period of unconditional captivity of Orthodox Theology by Western scholastic forms, our textbooks retold almost verbatim what was proclaimed in the Roman Catholic or Lutheran catechisms. Only at the end of the last century, in the famous lectures of Archimandrite Anthony Khrapovitsky, was this subject given a completely different direction. He brought this subject back to the writings of the Holy Fathers and the history of a true Orthodox tradition, resolutely shaking the dust of the dying and dry scholasticism.

Usually, the question of pastoral service is modified by moral standards, which, according to Archimandrite Anthony's precise remarks, "do not exceed the common obligatory requirements for all Christians, assuming that the pastor must be what every decent Christian ought to be." Initially, the indication usually points to the fact that the pastor must be prayerful, spiritual, must not be greedy for money, sober, meek and so forth. All these virtues are an essential requirement of the laity as well, yet obviously, these requirements should be more strictly applied to the pastor, since each of these virtues demands a higher degree of perfection. But this means that the difference between the virtues of the laity and pastoral moral perfection is merely one of quantity, not of essence. In other words, priesthood does not impart any special gifts upon the Christian. The contribution of Archimandrite, later Metropolitan, Anthony Khrapovitsky for the Russian school and Orthodox theology is the question he put before his listeners: "Does a special gift to the priesthood exist, and, if yes, what does it consist of?" Giving this question an interesting, original and certainly not a scholastically approved answer. This answer should by no means be accepted as absolute truth, which has no other possibly true answer, but which fully satisfies the Orthodox spirit of patristics and ascetical literature. It will be stated below that the imperfection of his opinion is an exposition, or more to the point, the doctrine of some Holy Fathers.

First of all, it must be kept in mind that in theological scholarship, Metropolitan Anthony was a strong advocate of psychology and morality. It shaped his master's degree work, *Psychological Grounds for the Benefit of Free Will and Moral Responsibility*; it shows through in all of his articles about moral applications of doctrines, and it also manifests itself in his famous *The Dogma of Redemption*. At that time, in the dominant age of positivism and determinism, such opinion was like a bright ray of sunshine and a breath of fresh air.

Psychology and morals accompanied him into pastoral theology as well. The calling, as was previously stated, definitely has no significance whatsoever; preparation, as stressed by Metropolitan Anthony, takes precedence over the spiritual-ascetic preparation. Self-exposure to pastoral attitudes and gifts requires a dedicated and deliberate attention, and this lecturer called particularly for an increase of this gift in one's self. The outline of this study, in its oversimplified form, may be directly linked to pastoral influence.

A person's will is free, but it is susceptible to the influence of a second will, affecting the will of that person to the extent of its inner significance. The power of this influence lies not so much in words and content, but in the persuasiveness of the spirit, morality and perfection. "Pastoral advocacy" — said Metropolitan Anthony — "is present in the Holy Scriptures as a power, acting independently of the very content of the sermon, but is dependent on the inner spirit of the speaker. Influences of the pastor's soul on his flock depends mainly on the degree of his devotion to his calling." The main stipulation of pastoral influence — he said — does not end in erudition, in psychological subtlety, or in moral personality, but in something else, which has no need for any mediation, in outward displays or in that which remains after all these displays are done with, but in an undetermined, innermost, not particularly well defined infusion into the soul of the speaker."

What is this special frame of mind, which can so influence the teacher? The gift of compassionate love — answers Metropolitan Anthony. This gift can give a new life to the fallen sinner, lift him out of the depths of despair and give him the strength for future moral improvement. It should not be forgotten that the very redemption of mankind itself depends, as is explained by this author, on the compassion for people in their sins, morally carrying their inner burdens and experiencing the loving and compassionate endurance of His Heart. Of course, this study of Christ's redemption of our race is concerned with the essence of moral suffering at Gethsemane; when the Lord prayed for this Cup to pass Him by, it was not the Cup of physical suffering on the Cross, but Christ's moral suffering for all mankind.

By using the worthwhile gift given to him, the pastor must strive in his work to identify himself spiritually with others, "assimilate his neighbor into himself, his heart,"[1] to extend his moral sense to his entire congregation. Through his own identification with the sinfulness of his congregation, his sympathy for their shortcomings, the pastor ideally must identify himself with others to such a degree that "I" now vanishes and only "We" remains. In other words, this study attempts to overcome isolation, subjectivity, independence and to reveal to a higher degree the common experiences and joys of all members of the Body of Christ.

In his teachings on "compassion" and "involvement," Metropolitan Anthony easily finds corroboration in Pauline epistles and the writings of some of the Fathers. Indeed, if, in the words of the Apostle, in contrast to the Old Testament, "we possess such a High Priest, Who can sympathize with our weaknesses (Hebrews 4:5), to which the Apostle adds, "My little children, for whom I labor in birth again until Christ is formed in you" (Galatians 4:19) or: "Who is weak and I am not weak?" (2 Corinthians 11:29) and

---

[1] *Collection of Essays*, p. 256.

even to strive for this, for, "I have become all things to all men, that I might by all means save some" (1 Corinthians 9:22).

To the degree that such a gift of sympathy is given to the priest in the Sacrament of "Laying on of the Hands" (*Chieratonia* or Ordination), Metropolitan Anthony finds a corroborating reference in St. John Chrysostom, whose comments on the Epistle to Colossians 11 state: "Special love does not give birth to anything earthy; it comes from on high, from heaven, and is given in the mystery of priesthood, but the assimilation and the maintenance of this benevolent gift depends on the striving of the human spirit." Similar thoughts may be found in St. John Chrysostom's other works, simply because this understanding of priesthood was characteristic of the great preacher and priest from Antioch.

Metropolitan Anthony also refers to the words of the Righteous Symeon the New Theologian who said: "He who has such love for God, that at the mere mention of Christ's name is immediately inflamed with so much love that he sheds tears and cries for his friends' and strangers' sins and considers himself to be the worst sinner of all" (*Words XII*). He also refers to the words of St. Tikhon of Zadonsk: "Love seeks to discover words with which to build up a friend."

To that we will add some of our own thoughts, which are found in the Holy Fathers. In his 28th letter to Sirius, St. Maximus the Confessor writes about the episcopal grace bestowed upon him, enabling him to become the initiator of blessings and be devoted to the gathering of the dispersed children of God and be united with them in the insoluble unity of spiritual love. St. Isaac the Syrian in his 8th "Words" wrote: "He who with compassion and without distinction loves everyone equally has attained perfection." Especially remarkable are his words about the "charitable heart," which "ignites in man a burning love for all creation; men, birds, animals, demons and every creature." The sight and remembrance of them brings tears to one's eyes. The great and powerful pity, a full heart and great sufferings squeeze his heart and he cannot bear, listen or look upon the smallest grief or harm inflicted on any creature. Therefore, he constantly and tearfully prays for the unenlightened, the enemies of God's truth and for those who do him harm, so that they may be forgiven and saved; he prays with great compassion as well for the life of all of nature's creatures.

These teachings of sympathizing with others were to a great degree extracted from the writings of Dostoyevsky, to which Metropolitan Anthony frequently and willingly referred and whose influence he acknowledged. Without doubt, to a considerable measure it revitalized our dry, scholastic and rationalistic study of pastoral science and inspired many a young priest in his sacrificial service to mankind. Of course, this increased the personal charm of the Metropolitan himself, who, by following and practicing these instructions, fulfilled the revival of the soul.

However, by itself, the study of the principles of sympathetic pastoral love and the assimilation of another person's conscience into the pastor's heart should not be construed as absolute. This alone does not comprise the spirit of pastoral service, but such a gift of love is, indeed, granted to the pastor in the mystery of the priesthood, his work is limitless. Theology is not merely asceticism; the priestly office is not limited to moralizing only; man's transfiguration is not accomplished by psychological absorption and the influence of one's will upon another.

Metropolitan Anthony wrote: "There is no pastoral work, only pastoral conscience." This, undoubtedly, is a difficult concept. If it is possible to say: "He who has no knowledge of Greek, no ear for music or does not possess an imposing personality and appearance is, however, not a bad pastor, but he who has not crushed his ego — an integral part of his life — who knows not how to pray, how to love, how to have compassion and to forgive, all these shortcomings nullify pastoral services."

Metropolitan Anthony Khrapovitsky was not himself inclined to draw extreme inference from this thesis. He did not identify Christianity with redemption only, not even monasticism. Quoting from the beautiful lines of our liturgical hymnography, taken from the texts of Psalms: "Filled with a somber and slavish sense of fear and a dread of torments beyond the grave," Metropolitan Anthony very eloquently examines the tendency of some pastors' preoccupation with coercive salvation, thereby misinterpreting the ancient history by stressing only the deeds of obedience, literally fulfilling only the approved responsibilities and rules. Such deeply religious and devout ascetics, who have little pastoral spirit, become oppressive autocrats to their flock.

Pastoral theology, undoubtedly, demands not only to enumerate various responsibilities and functions of the priest, but also to foster in him the pastoral spirit and frame of mind. It would be incorrect to limit this condition to compassion, psychological influence of one conscience upon another or to sermons about moral perfection only. In Metropolitan Anthony's theology, psychology and morals always suppress something, excluding especially all mysticism.

This moral element fits into the good news of Christianity and occupies its lawful place in all religious education. But this element cannot deplete all Christian spiritual life. Although the very Christian doctrine began with the words of the Forerunner, John the Baptist: "Repent, for the Kingdom of Heaven is at hand" (Matthew 3:2), the understanding of repentance contains two elements of Christianity: a negative and a positive element. The genius of the Greek language expresses this religious sense as being essentially different from our understanding of "repentance." In repentance, one can discern regret about a committed deed, remorse, something unfavorable, in a meaningful sense. Bitterness about irreparability occupies a principal place here. We do not hear in this word "do good" only "avoid evil." The Greek language does not contain such sadness about a committed wrong, but, to be exact, something impulsive, calling to new actions, inversely proportioned to what led to sin, since, literally, this word means "a change of mind" or, in a broader sense — "change of life, behavior, actions." Something energetic, constructive is heard in this appeal. The Apostle Paul's teaching is right to the point when he says: "Let a man so consider us, as servants of Christ and stewards of the mysteries of God" (1 Corinthians 4:1), or even more specifically: "And He Himself gave some to be apostles, some prophets, some evangelists, some pastors and teachers. For the equipping of the saints, for the work of ministry, for the edifying of the body of Christ" (Ephesians, 4:11–12). This moral, or more precisely, its spiritual element, assumes not only a sense of compassion and repentance for what had been done, which is useless in itself, but a sense of a new creation, a positive action and a full awareness of the Body of Christ and, therefore, it must be the doctrine of the Christian pastor and teacher. This mission is considerably greater than merely lamenting about one's sins, because repentance is not limited only to psychology and moralizing about bad actions, but to the creation of something positive and imperishable in the Heavenly Kingdom. The same Metropolitan Anthony, teaching about the pastoral influence of one conscience on another conscience, as well as about adoption of a foreign personality, until the creation of "I" is changed to "we" of pastoral love, did not intend to limit it to a negative condition of repentance, as it was pointed out earlier. To a considerable extent, the purely mystical element was obscured for him, which fully conformed to his rationalism and psychology.

How then can the words of the apostle about the establishment of mysteries be revealed? In what environment should the pastoral actions of the priest take its course? What can fill the one-sidedness and the exceptional psychological condition of the influence of one conscience upon another conscience? In the most important Christian mystery — we will answer — in the Eucharistic life, in the joining of the Eucharistic body to the mystical body of the Church. The Eucharistic life is, and should be, the main spiritual aspiration of the priest.

The priest, first and foremost, is a liturgist. Priesthood consists mainly of liturgy, Eucharist and the mystical union with Christ in the mystery of the Body and the Blood. This is the unity of the pastor and his flock. The spiritual life of the priest, first of all and most importantly of all, must be experienced in his own as well as his peoples' Eucharistically consecrated lives. The Eucharistic Church should, above all, envelop the priest. It is impossible for the Eucharist to exist outside of the Church and for the Church to exist without the Eucharist. The Church Fathers did not write treatises about the Church, but lived in her and by her, nor did they write in the classical theological scholastic period treatises about the Holy Spirit, but lived in the Spirit. The realization of the Mysteries is the way — the command to us from the Apostle Paul.

The fullness of the priest's service encompasses many responsibilities. The priest must answer to all demands presented to him by his calling. He is expected to teach, to feed the souls, do missionary work, perform the Divine Services, services for the sick, the imprisoned, the sorrowful, and many others, not to mention the modern Western passion for socializing, sports and other activities of the priest.

As to any other mere mortal, God may or may not have given the priest certain talents. He may be a bad orator or an incapable administrator of his parish, a poor teacher of Scriptures, may be even unfeeling and an excessively demanding spiritual leader, not to mention the fact that he may be completely lacking in skill for social service, but all this will be forgiven and will not erase his spiritual actions, if he would only possess a Eucharistic consciousness, if he will not cease to consider as his main mission the "concept of mysteries," the service of the Divine Liturgy, the mystical unity of self and his flock with the Body of Christ, "That through these you may be partakers of the Divine Nature" (2 Peter 1:4). If this same Metropolitan Anthony so remarkably called pastors "the path of prolonged heroic actions of the creation in self a prayerful element," as an ability to ascend to heaven, so by no means this element and this ability are to be accomplished in the priest except in the mystery of Eucharistic sacrifice.

But what do the Eucharistic frame of mind and the pastoral desire to serve the Divine Liturgy mean? Let us give here a clear and definite answer: an insatiable thirst to perform the Divine Liturgy as often as possible. Indeed, priesthood consists of the priest independently performing the Divine Liturgy, without concelebrating with another, be he a superior, archpriest, archimandrite or even a bishop. Concelebration prevents the concelebrants from performing this mystery of raising the Body of Christ. Concelebration quite often emphasizes the elements of solemnity, splendor, pomp and ritual rigor.[1] But, it must be pointed out, as much as the Holy Fathers wrote about prayers, they always spoke of the purity of prayer, its moderation; a wise prayer, *i.e.* its higher degree of spirituality, its boldness, and so forth, but never and

---

[1] Editors Note: Here Kern is referring to the hierarchical Divine Liturgy being shaped by the Byzantine imperial high court celebration with the use of eagle rugs and the various entrances and rites and rituals of Byzantium.

nowhere did any of the Holy Fathers or ascetics of the Church write of its pomposity. The very idea of pomposity and luxuriance stands in contrast to the Eucharistic vision of poverty and the spirit of Bethlehem and Golgotha. The pomp and splendor of communal pastoral service may be in accordance with the rituals of Byzantium and the Vatican's royal entrances and ceremonies, but is out of place at the Chalice of the Eucharistic Blood, poured out for the life of the world. One may speak of combined service and the receiving of communion from one chalice and from the hands of one priest or archpriest as encompassing all those around the priest, but it is not possible to speak about concelebration, because there is only one representative who serves, only one who symbolizes Christ, and the rest of the priests must be relegated to be assisting apostles, waiting for communion from the hand of the only one who serves. The history of the early Church, the history of liturgy, the writings of the early teachers of the Church, all teach us that the idea of a pompous ritual was to them totally foreign and incomprehensible.

Therefore, the priest must build up within himself a thirst for the individual performance of the Eucharistic service and not be content with a combined "situation," where he is surrounded by higher official representatives, be it bishops, archimandrites or archpriests. The priest must possess this insatiable thirst for Eucharistic service, which, of course, in no way belittles his thirst to receive communion from the hand of another, not necessarily older and higher ranking, colleague. But the mystical feeling, not understood by the laity, differs from the feeling of himself performing the sacrifice and creating, by the power of the Holy Spirit, gifts of the Body and the Blood, as opposed to the feeling and experience of receiving communion at a liturgy performed by another. The Eucharistic power given to the priest may be accurately measured by his thirst to serve unassisted. The most spiritual pastor always senses the pleasure of theistic prayer and service. As the late Father Sergius Bulgakov so brilliantly wrote in his *Autobiographical Notes*, "I entered the priesthood solely for the sake of serving, *i.e.* mainly to perform the liturgy. My naïve and inexperienced eye did not distinguish any details concerning the position of the parish priest. However, I understood very quickly that to serve, one needs a temple, or, at the very least, an altar. As a result, briefly speaking, for a quarter century of my priesthood, I did not have my own temple, but was always serving with either archpriests or senior priests, or had only an occasional chance for an independent service" (Chaps. 53–54). These lines, as well as other remarkable chapters in this outstanding book, portray exactly the yearning and thirst for his individual ceremonial service, independently performing the mystery, the raising of the Body of Christ. The point here is not humility, which some love to teach about and love to reproach the lack of the same, but simply a great, burning, fiery love for an active, priestly service, performed alone, rather than to be a passive co-attendant server, even with an older and perhaps a very worthy colleague.

The viewpoint on independently performing the Eucharistic mystery is our own personal opinion, no doubt with which many a priest will agree, but by no means will we call this the only and infallible understanding of the priestly service of the Divine Liturgy. We do not deny the Church accepted principle of a "combined" service, which undisputedly has its roots in antiquity. We only wanted to shed some light on the possibility that at the individual service, the priest may feel a more spontaneous and closer Eucharistic sacrifice experience than at a combined service.

It is necessary, however, to consider the result of the above-mentioned pastoral gifts and take into account its origin. At the mystery of ordination, the pastor receives a special gift, inaccessible to the laity: the reviving grace of the soul for the Kingdom of God. This revival grace may be transmitted to the flock by moral influence on its personality, by compassionate love for the sinners, by absorbing oneself into their personality, but most of all through the Eucharistic service and through the introduction of the believers to the mysteries of the body of the Church. The priest may not be the only one to influence morally those near to him: compassion may come from a mother and/or a teacher, absorption of another's personality can also be done by a close friend, but the Eucharistic service is given to the priest alone. The Divine Liturgy is a very powerful resource of pastoral service. Public prayers, funeral services, akathists cannot replace the Divine Liturgy. The priest must always remember that he is called to be the builder of God's mysteries, that the service of the Divine Liturgy and the administering of sacraments to the faithful are the most powerful tools of pastoral creative activities, through which the moral and mystical revival of man will be fulfilled.

CHAPTER 6

Preparation for the Priesthood

Occupying the central focal point throughout Christian history for the theological writers and ascetic teachers was the question of preparation for the future priest. For the sake of clarity, this question must be divided into several more specialized subjects of pastoral study courses. Mainly, it is divided into two parts:

1) Is the preparation for the highly-valued priestly service necessary, or must all such matters be entrusted to God's grace, which fills all and heals all?

2) What should this preparation consist of, if it is declared necessary?

In the latter case, this question be discussed alongside these special themes: spiritual preparation, intellectual preparation and external preparation. By taking a routine look at this question, one may see two opposite opinions. According to one theory, no human science, specialization or skill can, nor should, take place where the bounty of the Holy Spirit is sought; it is omnipotent, and, therefore, sufficient. The other theory is exactly the opposite. Preparation is essential; therefore, it should be painstaking, elaborate and extensive. If, according to one opinion, the priest should comply with the most necessary and simple requirements of commonly and primitively understood liturgical piety, then, according to our wise and observant Bishop Porfirii Uspensky, it would be limited to the "censer and the sprinkling brush," since, as many tend to think, "for the sake of humility," more would not be required; yet, according to the other opinion, the preparation of the future priest should be broad enough to impose upon him a duty to understand the simple households of a village as well as medical disciplines and other various practical subjects (*i.e.* regulations of our religious schools, established in 1839, as well as the regulations of Serbian religious seminaries in the period between the wars of 1914 and 1938), the sports of today, the ability to lead youth camps as well as modern social concerns.

Therefore, pastoral study must find an equilibrium and discover that middle "royal golden" road, so that the priest could avoid primitivism and obscurity, yet would not be excessively absorbed by completely uncharacteristic pastoral concerns.

After these introductory remarks, we must now turn to the first question, namely, is preparation for priesthood necessary? The answer suggests itself to be in the affirmative. This is instilled into us by the entire history of priesthood and the collective experience of the Church. It is true that in the past ages of Christianity, religious schools did not always exist — yet pastoral preparation was always required. On the other hand, at a time of great tranquility in the Church. The hierarchy did not support systematic education. History acknowledges the famous schools of Alexandria, Odessa, Constantinople, Rome and many various other places in the first centuries of the Church's existence. The age of great religious debates and the emergence of heresies provided the Church with a keener sense for the necessity of preparation. If in the first three centuries a systematic religious and pastoral education was not in existence, then, from the time of recognition of Christianity as a free state religion, its education became more and more organized and was vastly improved.

It did not always have the same forms: monasteries were the center of education for a long time; occasionally, prominent individual hierarchs or pastors assembled future priests around themselves; such was the priestly preparation in the period of the enslavement of the Church by the Tatars and the Turks and in neglected and remote countries, removed from the main centers of civilization. But it may definitely be asserted that the Church had never given up paying attention to this question, cautiously admitting young candidates to priesthood by the laying on of the hands and requiring of them a sound, knowledgeable and multifaceted preparation.

Among the widespread misunderstanding about Christianity, there undisputedly exists the most dangerous notion of all, one that depicts Christianity as a religion of simpletons, ignorant and uneducated people. This was maintained by Emperor Julian the Apostate and the famous Celsus, stemming from their hostile feelings toward Christianity and a desire to humiliate it, yet the works of St. John Chrysostom, Gregory the Theologian, Basil the Great, Photius, and many others are full of quotations from a great variety of written sources, such as Ecclesiastes, Saints as well as pagan authors. People of our time, devoted Christians, also love to maintain this notion, but instead of preserving Christianity's purity, simplify and redeem it.

As was pointed out earlier, the Cave of the Incarnate Birth was visited not only by simple shepherds, but wise men from the East, seeking God, bearing God's highest truth beyond the world of Christianity. If, on the one hand, the Savior called simple fishermen, then, on the other hand, among the people who most of all spread Christianity, was Apostle Paul, an educated man of his time. Very early on, Christianity recognized intellectuals and defenders, such as the holy Martyr Justin the Philosopher, Athenagoras, Clement of Alexandria, not to mention the galaxy of ecumenical teachers and pastors of the golden age of the Church.

It should be remembered that the Apostle Paul, author of the Epistles, relentlessly put many great requirements upon his students and coworkers and issued guiding instructions for the appropriate examination of those who sought ordination at the hands of a bishop. The apostle warns: "do not lay hands on anyone hastily" (1 Timothy 5:22); he demanded that besides moral qualities, the bishop should also "be able to teach" (1 Timothy 3:2); and requiring that they "be tested" (1 Timothy 3:10). The clergyman constantly has to admonish "with all authority" (Titus 2:15), "in season and out of season" (2 Timothy 4:2); "to continue in the things you have learned and been assured of" (2 Timothy 3:14), "holding fast the faithful word as he has been taught, that he may be able, by sound doctrine, both to exhort and convict those who contradict" (Titus 1:9), "these things command and teach" (1 Timothy 4:11), "take heed to yourself, and to the doctrine."

If we proceed from the apostolic writings to the works of the teachers of the classical period of our theology, we will easily find confirmation on what we said about intellectual preparation. Those advocates who vainly seek to oversimplify and obfuscate Christianity, allude to examples of some Christian pastors, like Bishop Severus — a former mill worker, and Alexander — a coal miner. These cases do not represent the accepted rule and are the exceptions from the common majority, and are, therefore, difficult to find in the history of priesthood. The Church demanded something else. The lessons learned from the mouths of the Church's best and most experienced teachers direct the priest, and especially the bishop, not only to practice piety, but to study and acquire wisdom from reading, a practice that will become, with the passing of years and the growing dangers for the Church, a greater and deeper experience. It must always be kept in mind that the direction of the Church, like a ship, was corrected in its most critical, troubled times of heresies and schisms, by the hands of loyal, experienced and wise helmsmen. Yet, the temptations of primitivism and obfuscation were apparently always hovering around the priesthood. Not in vain did many prominent writers of the Church warn those seeking the priesthood about the difficulties of this art, elevating it above sciences and human wisdom. There exists an interesting legend about an episode in the life of Pope Leo the Great who had a vision shortly before his death, in which the Apostle Peter announces the forgiveness of all his sins, save one: the sin of rash and careless ordinations of priests. Then, in a second vision, after the Pope's special prayers, forgiveness for this sin is granted as well.

It is, therefore, quite natural that the great teachers and priests of the ecumenical Church repeatedly uttered words of warning or reproach for careless treatment of admittance to the priesthood for those who sought it and for those who administered the laying of the hands. To such luminaries as St. John Chrysostom belong the famous *Six Books of the Priesthood*, to St. Ambrose of Milan *The Responsibilities of the Clergy* and to Blessed Jerome *About the Life of the Clergy*, works that are revered as guiding and warning instructions for future pastors of the Church. Pope St. Gregory the Dialogist wrote also about the responsibilities of priests. Brilliant words on the same subject came also from St. Ephraim the Syrian and Gregory the Theologian, who, as is well known, was forced into ordination by his father and, fearing the high calling of the priesthood, withdrew into the wilderness. His 42nd, or defensive, letter represents an explanation of his flight and at the same time a confession about how he views the life and activities of a priest; therefore, this letter can and should serve as a highly edifying guide for priests.

This is what St. John Chrysostom writes: "... accept ignorant men as priests and appoint them to oversee property for which the Son of God paid with His Blood. We pervert priesthood by entrusting it to inexperienced people." There is an often-heard opinion that preparation hinders piety, holiness, humility and so forth; therefore, it would not be remiss in this instance to cite the words of the Blessed Jerome: "Ignorant and simple priests consider themselves holy, because they do not know anything." St. Gregory the Theologian (3rd letter) warns: "First one must gain wisdom, then teach wisdom" or "one cannot be a worthless model for other painters"; "we do not have an established boundary between teaching and studying"; "it is one thing to be a shepherd of sheep and bullocks, and quite another thing to direct human souls." In subsequent years, those teachers and archpriests who understood the dangers of quick and untested ordinations would not still their voices. St. Tikhon of Zadonsk, as well as Holy Father John of Kronstadt, wrote about preparation and it was extensively covered, as mentioned in the first chapter, in Pastoral Theology courses. It should also be remembered that certain pastoral teachers, Metropolitan Anthony, for one, while denying the necessity of the so-called calling, transferred the center of gravity to the question of preparation.

In pre-revolutionary Russia, the general education for the priesthood consisted of ten years, four years of religious school and six years of seminary; those desiring a higher level of preparation had to go through another four-year course at a theological academy, so that the full education was acquired over the span of fourteen years. The Catholic world also has minor and major seminaries and faculties of theology which correspond to our theological academies. In some particular cases, such as in a post-war period, in times of upheavals or in far-flung regions, it was necessary to revert, as a last resort, to shortened pastoral courses, but this was only the exception to the general rule. Returning to the question of what comprises pastoral preparation for the priest's future activities, we must break up this subject into three parts.

SPIRITUAL PREPARATION. The priestly candidate, the future pastor, is preparing to embark upon a spiritual path, or, according to Russian terminology, enter the priesthood. This word alone commits us to a great deal. It does not fully cover its similar terminology in other languages; "*Sveshtenstvo*" (Serbian); "*Klir, Clerge,* Clergy" (Greek, French, and English), but corresponds more to the German understanding of "*Geistlicher,*" from "*Geist,*" spirit. First of all, the clergy must be spiritual. It signifies a belonging to the Kingdom of the Spirit, not to the Kingdom of social commitments, the domain of materialistic calculations and interests, political desires, and so forth. This, before all else, means the education of self in the Spirit of the Kingdom of God, of creation of it within self, for this Kingdom is not somewhere, in some earthly dominion, but in us. The Kingdom of God is not a theocratic idea, but a category of our spirituality. This is the first requirement on the path of spiritual education, a spirit, which, it is sad to say, is often absent in the clergy, a clergy that is inflamed with passions of national and political aspirations, or even weighed down with cares about daily bread and with seeking material goods. This spiritual growth does not occur all at once, but is acquired by long-standing inspirations, spread over one's whole life: spiritual self-education from early childhood and a decisive choice of directing one's aspirations — to the earthly kingdom or to that which is not of this world.

Two elements in this choice become clear — a negative and a positive element. The first one leads to a decisive rejection of all things that are of this world and draw us to it; the sin of seeking earthly gains, career motivations, national political biases and so forth. This does not at all denote an aversion for cultural and social participation, but rather a release from all attractions of this world, its evils, its non-spiritual impulses. This means not being a slave to worldly concerns, to all that is sinful. The positive element consists of accumulating all that is spiritual, all that is characteristic of the grace of the Kingdom. It must be developed; it stands at the forefront of this goal. According to St. Gregory the Theologian, the pastor must be heavenly, that is, he must not be involved with worldly sins and be a prisoner of its material goods. The pastor must be holy, yet this does not mean some pseudo-spiritual puritanism or some dried-up, anemic spirituality, memorizing special buzzwords and Church Slavonic expressions, sanctimonious parading and hypocrisy, but a genuine spirituality, that is, striving for God's adoption and nurturing this spirituality and devotion in self and others, in order to be able to rise to a higher ideal of Orthodox asceticism. The pastor must be kind and compassionate, which does not at all mean sentimental, but the ability to assimilate with himself the joys, sins, sorrows and suffering of others. The pastor must be vulnerable, that is, become like Christ, Who is the perfect ideal of the Good Pastor. The pastor must be prayerful, that is, loving the activity of prayer in all its forms, especially the private prayer, the Jesus Prayer, praying in Church and most of all the services of Divine Liturgy. A priest without prayer, incapable of praying, not willing to explore the elements of prayer, not attracted to liturgy and in every way, under all plausible and implausible pretexts avoiding it, is a contradiction to himself and an unproductive administrator of spirituality. The pastor must be humble, that is, devoid of a sense of pride, arrogance, conceit, ambition, vanity and egoism. Humility is not expressed by low bows before others and not at all by signing ones name with the designation of "humble priest so-and-so," nor by putting self into the center of the whole world, self-admiration, but in a genuine liberation from all egocentrism.

The list of priestly qualifiers could be extended. All of the above may be reduced to a single condition — spirituality — that is, freedom from the power of any sin as well as any worldly, nationalistic and political ambitions. Now we should turn to the means of this spiritual education.

It would not be incorrect to state that the most powerful means to attain spirituality is in prayer. It alone is the very sphere of spiritual life, and besides, thanks to prayer, other spiritual blessings, previously lacking, may be obtained in prayer. The candidate must learn how to pray during his school days. By observing whether the future priest loves the Divine Liturgy or avoids it, the directions of his striving can be judged accordingly; will the act of prayer be borne as a heavy burden or will the time spent in prayer become the best minutes of his life. This should not be generalized, since the ability to pray is a very individual matter. For some, prayer in Church, conventionally arranged and ascetically more attractive, seems closer to the soul, while for others the public Church prayer is much harder than a private, innermost prayer of the heart. Therefore, the step to be taken next is: reading the Holy Scriptures, memorizing them, reflecting upon them, deepening the mind through understanding of the Scriptures, familiarizing oneself with expository literature, literature of the Holy Fathers as well as contemporary literature. Moreover, to cultivate spiritual growth, a general knowledge of the works of the Holy Fathers, mainly in their ascetic forms, is required and should be used as a guide to moral perfection, because these works were written not from theoretical opinions, but from many years' experiences of desert and monastic life. To accomplish this goal, there has to be a gradual reading preparation, beginning with the simpler writings, such as those of Sts. Abba Dorotheus, John of Kronstadt, Theophan the Recluse and Ignatius Brianchaninov; the letters of Ambrose of Optina, and gradually advancing to more difficult study, as, for example, *The Philokalia*, Isaac the Syrian, *The Ladder of Divine Ascent*, Symeon the New Theologian and Gregory Palamas.

A vital means for spiritual preparation for the priesthood could take the form of frequent confessions, spiritual debates with knowledgeable people, the reading of famous spiritual biographies and prayer books. The Western world is familiar with certain lengthy exercises in prayer and contemplations practiced in monasteries. Such solitary and private, concentrated exercises of fasting substantially edify and build-up the spiritual wealth of the soul.

Participation in the course of spiritual preparation may include some of the following: visiting the sick, helping the suffering humanity and coming to the aid of anyone who suffers and is in need of compassion. It may be helpful to focus one's thoughts not on this transient, "beautiful world," but on the elements of death, eternity and life after death. The reading of the Psalter over the deceased also may greatly enhance the young candidate's preparation for the priesthood.

Summarizing all of the above: it is imperative in the process of fostering the spiritual growth of the priest, to involve the cultivation of those traits that are helpful in renouncing compulsory laws and customs of this world, and to obtain the virtues that are conducive for the future priest to become spiritual and holy. All this contains within itself a special discipline, known as pastoral asceticism.

Intellectual Preparation. First of all, the harmful and deeply ingrained prejudice, that the pastor does not need intellectual preparation, as well as the claim that such preparation is allegedly harmful and can interfere with humility, the life of prayer and spirituality, must be overcome and absolutely renounced. This is one of the most dangerous delusions in society as well as among the clergy, clergy that are the primary guides of future priests. Here we have intentionally raised the matter of the three points of preparation in hierarchical order: spiritual, intellectual and external, so that once and for all we can declare that, without spiritual preparation and spiritual aspiration, the priest is merely an empty name, a self-contradiction, false and unworthy. Therefore, in this given context, we insist once more: without doubt, the pre-eminent place belongs to spiritual self-preparation and after that comes everything else. At this point, it is necessary to emphasize that spiritual self-preparation in no way impedes other intellectual and external developments; modern-day reality insistently demands the highest pastoral preparation possible and the widest intellectual range of interests as well as common courtesy and other general skills. The objection to the statement that any intellectual and external preparation which comes in contact with culture and service can harm and even destroy the pastor's spirituality is bolstered by the fact that such spirituality is insignificant and not worth a great deal. It must be remembered that Orthodox spirituality is not as fragile as many fear.

Turning once more to history, past examples provide rich material to bring this matter to a favorable resolution. In fact, the Fathers of the classical era of Orthodox theology — St. Athanasius, the Cappadocians, St. Maximus the Confessor, Patriarch Photius, St. John of Damascus and many others, were representatives of a very wide intellectual culture of their time. They represented the highest elite strata of their time. Their writings contain evidence that their education derived not only from Scripture and the Holy Fathers who preceded them, but from expert testimony of pagan writers as well. They were perfectly familiar with philosophy, rhetoric, mathematics and music, that is, all that, in the academic world of that day was known as "the seven arts," or *trillium* and *quadrillium*. What is also quite amazing, is that at no time did they fear that by giving the undisputed precedence to spiritual preparation and piety, secular education could somehow interfere with their piety and spirituality. Indeed, neither was their humility, faith nor prayer life impeded by their familiarity with Plato, Aristotle, Homer, Virgil, and so forth. Those who would dwell even a little deeper into the study of patristic writings and read the Holy Fathers could not help but wonder at the high level and standard of education of those whom they would present as simpletons and obfuscators. Obfuscators and simpletons are exactly how the enemies of Christianity, such as Lucian, Celsius and Julius the Apostate wished to present them, yet the Holy Fathers surprised even the pagans with their external, that is, intellectual preparation. The biographies of saints and ascetic anthologies were not the only works preserved in monastic libraries. For example, it is interesting to note that St. Athanasius, a sophisticated Hellenist and expert on his own language, used expressions found only in the seldom read works, such as studies on Euripides and Aristophanes. In order to remember such subtle linguistic points, these books must be read with great attention, which perhaps today would be considered out of place for monastic reading. Inferences may be made even in our own time from familiarity with the times of Plutarch and Plotinus. Knowledge of modern philosophy, literature, sciences and arts can only elevate the pastor's stature in the eyes of those of his flock who wish to learn from the priest about one or another cultural phenomenon. For the priest, such knowledge can be quite useful ammunition in his missionary and apologetics work. Only then can the pastor influence his flock, when he knows its heartbeat and what most attracts it. The priest's spirituality will not suffer from his familiarity with modern philosophical and literary trends. The price of that spirituality, which can suffer from contact with philosophy or be diminished by knowledge of literature, is not very great indeed. All intellectual preparation first of all implies a deep and genuine spirituality on the part of the priest. Intellectual preparation in no way should be a pretext for pastoral worldliness.

It is imperative to remember the potential cultural influence upon society. A society that is left by its pastor to its own devices and chances of fate in its growth and educational opportunities, becomes easy prey to outside pressures and matures without the rewarding and guiding influence of a priest. No genuinely cultured person will turn to a priest who either knows nothing about modern matters or looks contemptuously away from anything that does not represent his narrow specialty of liturgy, required duties of the Church and elementary sermons. People expect authoritative and well-thought-out answers, wise and knowledgeable, that originate from a well-educated mind. Orthodox clergy, by virtue of many historical and social reasons, could not, or quite often did not know how to create this influence or how to stay ahead of the cultural process. In France, the clergy were the creation of this cultural class and listened to it. The Russian Academy of Science admitted such personalities as Metropolitan Filaret, Metropolitan Makary Bulgakov, and Platon Levshin, as well as some priests such as Koschetov, Archimandrite Polycarp Goitannikov and Gerasim Pabsky. This, of course, viewed as a purely formal indication, cannot limit the cultural-educational factor among the clergy. Yet, even by expanding these parameters, the same experienced guidance in cultural matters, such as is exhibited in the countries of Western Europe, cannot be observed in the Orthodox clergy.

These examples can, without putting an undue stress on memory, only attest to the fact that enlightened priests were not at all the last ones in promoting the movement of spiritual progress and pastoral care. It is sufficient to remember such thinkers as Archpriest Theodore A. Golubinsky, Archimandrite Theophan Avsenev and Archbishop Nikanor Brovkivich, Famous Sinologists such as Archimandrite Avakum the Sanctified and Palladin Kafarov; Hebraist Father Gerasim Pavliky, Bishop Porfirii Uspensky and Archimandrite Anthony Kapustin — all great Russian Byzantine scholars and leading experts on the Greek and Russian languages. Archimandrite Anthony and his brother Platon Kapustin, one of the famous Moscow priests of his time, were good astronomers, and Fr. Platon wrote articles on higher mathematics. The last Protopresbyter of the Uspensky Cathedral in pre-revolutionary Russia, Fr. N. A. Lubimov, held a master's degree in Russian literature, teaching this subject at the famous Fisherov Gymnasium, Fr. I. Fudel, a great friend of Constantine Leontiev and a man of letters, has also taught law at this Gymnasium; our priests, living in foreign lands, became members of Academic Societies of Germany, Sweden, Spain and England.

Serving as an example in the Russian past is Archimandrite John Mikhailovich Pervushin, prior of the Village Church in Mekhonsk, in the Perm province (+June 16, 1900), a humble and prayerful priest, a kind and thoughtful pastor, who, besides all this, was also a remarkable mathematician, famous in the world of mathematics. Upon graduating from the Kazan Theological Academy, he went to a rural Church, where he spent the rest of his life. Gifted with exceptional mathematical ability, he began to send his work to the Academy of Sciences and was acquainted not only with the prominent mathematicians of Russia, but with those of the Western world as well. His mathematical and numerical theories were rewarded by our Academy and were registered in the Mathematical Congress in Chicago and the Neapolitan Physics–Mathematical Society. The numerical theories did in no way prevent him from being a good priest.

If desired, the list can be expanded, but it is important to remember that neither a title as a member of Academic Sciences, studies of astronomy, philosophy and/or Byzantium, nor any other display of erudition and education can impede a spiritual individual to be liturgical, an excellent pastor and a humble monk, whose main calling is to exert a great spiritual influence upon his flock.

There is no greater lie and slander that is leveled at Orthodox spirituality than grouping it with obfuscation and Gnosticism. Obfuscating inclinations among some clergy should in no case be applied to all Orthodoxy. Orthodoxy has nothing to do with it.

It is also imperative to remember that in times such as ours, when the enemies of the Church are mobilizing all their forces to fight against her, the presence of enlightened pastors, steeled by scientific schooling, who are always ready to "answer" to our "hope," according to the Apostle Peter, is more than appropriate. The pastor is expected to confess fearlessly, and therefore humbly, his own incompetence, yet to use the words, "by power" forcefully and with authority. Since our clergy are not accustomed to, nor wish to be leaders in these matters, it is not surprising that those seeking guidance in life, turn to people who are far removed from spirituality and the Church. The intelligentsia's inherent lack of spirituality may be cured to a considerable extent by spirituality's approach to its strivings and interests.

Turning once more to the modern reality, it must be remembered that the great influence exerted upon society by Metropolitan Anthony, Frs. Sergius Bulgakov, Alexander Elchaninov and G. Spassky is explained by the fact that they had an excellent knowledge of secular literature and kept up with arts, sciences and current thoughts.

Throughout history, elements that may be helpful or harmful can be found within all secular education. From Plato and Homer, the Church Fathers extracted those elements that could bring enlightenment to their time, but avoided those in pagan education, which were unnecessary and confusing. This matter is not solely a concern of this or any other century; the danger is not confined to the present or ancient times. Metropolitan Filaret of Moscow wrote at the time (August 27, 1858): "They wage war against contemporary ideas, yet are not the ideas of Orthodoxy and morality the essence of contemporary ideals? Have they only remained in the past? Are all of us pagans? The time is not at fault; immoral and unorthodox ideas, circulated by some people, are. Thus, the fight must be directed against unorthodox and immoral, not contemporary, ideas."[1] "It is futile to yearn for the past, since no escape from the perils of the present time can be found there," Metropolitan Filaret wrote to the Superior of the Trinity Monastery, Archimandrite Anthony on March 29, 1838: "The nineteenth century cannot be transformed into the fourth or fifth century, any more than the Vologoda province can be converted into the Thebaid province."[2] In any case, our great prelates understood the benefit of education and were always able to defend Orthodoxy from attacks and accusations of obfuscation. To Metropolitan

---
[1] *Collections of Views and Opinions*. Book IV, chapter 344.
[2] *Letters to the Superior of the Monastery*, Book 1, p. 315.

Isidor of Novgorod, he wrote: "In vein does the critic think that the Christian faith is hostile to knowledge, because it is not in union with ignorance."[1]

The pastor, of course, has to be very well aware of the dangers that lie in his path. With enthusiastic desire to be cultured and erudite, the priest may easily yield to the temptation of secularization and, imperceptibly, put the wrong appraisal on intellectual values. When the pastor begins to lose his primary and only need, when literature, philosophy and a compassionate care for his flock are disrupted, the pastor has lost his way. Therefore, involvement with the secular must always be tempered by a degree of a prayerful, pastoral frame of mind and purely spiritual aspirations. The goal of priestly life and actions is to create spirituality in self and in those close to him; intellectual and secular education may only be used as a means for pastoral influence as well as to enhance his own inner well being. The pastor should not fear education, but must in every way possible beware of being distracted by it to the detriment of his spirituality, because achieving perfection on the spiritual level is much harder than on the mental, artistic and scientific levels. Besides, the only correct course of action is the middle of the road and is only possible when one is in full harmony and balance with all the other competing forces.

---

[1] *Collections of Opinions and Beliefs*, Book V, p. 48.

EXTERNAL PREPARATION. Not the least of mistakes is the conviction that the pastor has no need for external education. In an effort to oversimplify and vulgarize Orthodoxy, some are prepared to be easily reconciled with the external uncouthness of the clergy, even perceiving in it some kind of a positive quality. In the absence of respect, elementary external decorum and lack of good manners, some quite often seek the anchor of salvation in the imaginary humility. One should not, however, take the trouble to try to prove that the Christian virtue of humility has nothing in common with rudeness and external lack of self-control. To the unprejudiced observer, it should become quite clear that genuine humility in no way suffers from cleanliness, good breeding and good manners. One should also not assume that ascetic, pious and humble people are boorish, uncouth morons. It is difficult to imagine St. Gregory the Theologian, St. Photius of Constantinople or St. Maximus the Confessor in the days of old, or the Blessed Seraphim, the Elder Ambrose of Optima or Bishop Theophan the Recluse of our own time, to hide under the cover of rudeness and indiscipline for the sake of preserving their humility and the fear of losing their spiritual goals. The distortion of the Christian spirit stems from the words of Tertullian, who, bent on his rigorous monasticism, claims that "to God the purity of the soul is far more important than the cleanliness of the body." It remains quite incomprehensible, why would the use of soap and a toothbrush diminish the purity of our soul?

What then does this external preparation consist of and to what should the priest direct his attention, in order to constantly behave with the proper external decorum?

a) External appearance consideration: The pastor must always keep in mind that "the clothes make the man." External appearance is enormously important in communal life. At first glance, some seemingly minor and inappropriate external details can alienate people. It is a human characteristic, inherent in man from birth, to be squeamish, and so because of it he cannot force himself to overlook a number of external trivialities, such as neatness and reputation. The priest should never fail to take this into account. By not paying attention to the seemingly insignificant trifles, he will lose something much more important: the ability to attract an exacting person. Consequently, the pastor must painstakingly care for his external appearance, that is always being neat and clean in regard to the his clothes as well as the body. The over-cassock and under-cassock must be in good repair, neat and always clean. No one would reproach a priest for meagerness of clothing, but its untidiness may alienate the people around him. Furthermore, a rich silk or moiré cassock could also provoke a highly unfavorable impression, giving rise to accusations of foppishness and dandyism. Poor clothes can never be used as a reproach to the priest, if he wears them with dignity and keeps them neat and tidy. Shoes, even if old, should always be in good repair and polished.

Proper attention should also be given to the cleanliness of hands, face, and teeth. Touching upon such minute details in the pastoral theological courses may seem strange and trivial, yet not everyone understands what a great significance such cleanliness holds for parishioners and worshipers. Dirt under the fingernails, unwashed ears and bad breath can repel quite a few unapproving worshipers who are sensitive to such things. Indeed, it takes quite a great deal of inner discipline and an utter absence of fastidiousness, let us say, at the time of confession, to be standing in the immediate vicinity of a person who emanates a foul odor or reeks of tobacco or garlic.

The rigorously conservative attitude of Russian priests and all Eastern clergy in general concerning long hair and beards should be tempered by fundamental requirements of basic cleanliness. Since long hair is not an essential canonical requirement for identifying one as a member of the Orthodox clergy; it must be noted that their unkempt appearance simply repels a cultured contemporary person. There existed in the Spiritual Consistory, during the reign of Empress Elizabeth, an order that the priests could not have their hair cut by a barber; this procedure was to be performed only by their wives. Our clergy, serving in foreign lands, always retained the right to have their hair cut by barbers. Church regulations clearly instruct them to trim "shaggy whiskers." Otherwise, there is a tendency, which is highly improper and unaesthetic, to suck on ones mustache, not only at meals, but at the Eucharist as well. Moderately cut hair, a trimmed beard and fairly short whiskers in no circumstances can reduce the priest's spirituality or give ground for reproach of foppishness.

All of the above mentioned in regard to external cleanliness, can, of course, as everything else, turn easily into the opposite extreme, when the priest's attention to his external appearance borders on dandyism and exaggeration.

b) Time consideration: The priest must be punctual in planning his business talks, visitations and services. A lack of punctuality is characteristic of the majority of easterners, especially Slavs, a characteristic which, more than anything else, irritates busy people who are always mindful of their time. The priest must live according to a rigid schedule. His day must be calculated in minutes; all business appointments scheduled, all periods of time taken into account. Liturgy must begin punctually at the appointed time. No changes should ever take place to accommodate someone or another who is late. Only at the time of mortal danger, being called to the bedside of a gravely ill person or to baptize an ailing infant may the priests be permitted to break their usual schedules. The priest is duty-bound to cultivate this spirit in self and, under his guidance, to expect the same actions from his flock. Such are the stipulations of social discipline.

c) Language and motion considerations: The word of the priest, much more than that of a simple mortal, attracts everybody's attention. By words do we judge the substance of one's inner thoughts and feelings. A loose tongue denotes an undisciplined mind; a bitter word gives evidence of being enslaved by an ill temper; coarse words reveal a lack of good breeding. Conversely, strict, restrained and well-defined words, words that are seasoned with good-natured humor, expose an intellectual mind, a mind that does not lack the powers of observation and at the same time possesses an inborn, easy-going cheerfulness. On the one hand, a loose and coarse speech, acquired in early school days and abounding in youthful jargon, may slip, even against one's will, easily and imperceptibly from the tongue, much more than is allowed by social standards. Regrettably, this tendency is often observed in our hierarchs. However, one psychological detail should be noted: Unrestricted, coarse speech may often be taken as evidence of some epic, irresistible, unconsciously driven underground fear, as if in defense of some kind of a chaste, timid protected flower. On the other hand, however, the young priest, for the sake of some falsely understood stylization of a far-fetched Orthodox-inspired spirituality, develops a kind of pseudo-sacred language, such as: "Save, O Lord" — instead of the usual "I thank you," "I am much obliged," "I, the great sinner," — instead of the common "I," "your sacredness," "I, the accursed," "I, much humiliated," and other epithets used because of self-consciousness of the neophyte priest in his belief that such expressions are signs of spirituality and humility. Reference should be also made here to the passion to flaunt appropriately and inappropriately Slavic quotations from the Bible and liturgical books, which are proper at times and which tend to season and enliven one's speech, but more often than not are artificial, deliberate, forced and at some point simply out of place.

The priest should develop in self a certain intrinsic inner rhythm of gestures and stride, which, nevertheless, must conform to his calling. Running around the streets is not appropriate for the priest's office, but a pompous appearance makes him look comical and denotes a poor grasp of his role. Extravagant arm gestures coarsen his manner, but a stiff appearance indicates an unnatural tautness. In the presence of a senior colleague, the priest should always remember his place; that is — not to sit down before permission has been given, to walk to the left of his superior, to always yield the way, etc. When traveling by train or by bus, he should not be in a hurry to occupy a seat. Should it, however, be offered to him, the priest may take it, but he must always endeavor to cede it to the old, the sick, the weak and women with children.

d) Correspondence considerations: There should be an immediate response to each letter, or at least fittingly communicated information. Letters should always be dated, yet better still, they should be numbered; it may be helpful to keep copies of business papers and other correspondence to avoid a later misunderstanding and forgetfulness. Letters written to higher-standing hierarchical clergy should be formal, concise and compact, without any familiarity. The signature must also be according to established form, without unnecessary "multi-sinner," "unworthy" and other disparaging and pseudo-humble epithets. The language of the letter, more than the spoken word, must be clear and correct. Generally, it must always be kept in mind that the consequences of one or another word or action could result in blushing and shame.

e) Housekeeping consideration: Housekeeping is very important; it can cause a positive or a negative reaction to the priest in the eyes of his parishioners. Order and neatness of a home was a subject in the pastoral Epistle of the Apostle Paul (1 Timothy 1:4–5). Poverty can never be used as a reproach, but disorder or excessive worldliness may seduce many. The weakness of the human spirit and its easy predisposition to temptation must always be kept in mind. Besides, one should never forget about the great impression the first look leaves behind. In addition to rudimentary cleanliness, the pastor's living quarters should reflect the interests and inner disposition of its owner. The opportunity open to the priest to acquire books and to develop a love for them will draw the attention of the cultured and the erudite. Wall decorations, whether illustrations, portraits or works of art reproductions, should not offend the aesthetic sense of visitors. It is quite wrong to think that the priest's room must be adorned with "pious" images, be they ever so pleasing, yet obviously offensive to the artistic sense of those knowledgeable in art. All that is trite, petty, stereotyped and market-driven may evoke a smile and a suspicion in the visitor's mind of the owner's desire to imitate the common cultural examples. Deviations of excessive worldliness and imitations of a far-fetched, stylized image of the "contemporary priest," the original having long ago vanished from life, and really no longer needed, can pose great dangers for the priest.

In conclusion, one more thing needs to be said — perhaps the most important one — that it is imperative to develop in self an inner spiritual flair, tact, a keen ear and a "quick eye" in order to be able to determine the proper way of action and to set an example which will benefit any one given occasion and situation.

CHAPTER 7

Ordination

The most important and the most awesome moment in the life of every priest, a moment which shall remain in his memory for the rest of his days, even unto his death, is when the bishop lays his hands upon his head for his ordination to the Holy Priesthood. In the previous chapter, a lot was said about the protracted scholastic preparations for pastoral work. The future priest must carefully examine his frame of mind, so that in the last days of his earthly life it may be in accord with his high calling and may enable him to draw nearer to the very mystery of priesthood.

In his last academic term at seminary, the candidate is faced with the crucial question about his future parish, that altar to which the Church will appoint him as its pastor.[1] Although this question is not a part of pastoral theology *per se*, but rather a canonical matter, it is nevertheless imperative to say a

---

[1] Editor's note: Here Kern is referring to the last academic term in seminary.

few words about these formal administrative details, since they cannot help but be of concern for the future priest.

There are three known models of ministry in the history of Christianity. The Protestant approach, which basically should not even be mentioned, since it has neither ordination nor priesthood nor any sign of a formal Church, an approach, which deviates into one extreme; dissidents from Rome confine themselves to one selected community. This is sufficient in the eyes of those who acquired their freedom from the Roman prelate and the distorted teachings of the Church by buying delusions of sanctification of self and others with the price of Presbyterian anarchy, where the blessed elements are completely dismissed. This is the extreme democratization of the Church.

On the other hand, the Roman Catholic approach went to the opposite extreme, by way of utter suppression, at least in principle, with very few exceptions, of affirmation of individuality, the source of the world and its very people. In the Roman understanding, the Church is concentrated in its hierarchy. That royal priesthood, which is chosen by the people and about which both the Old and the New Testaments speak, was not forgotten in early Christianity, yet has been completely obscured in the consciousness of the high ranking Roman prelates. The people do not take part in the elections of its clergy. The ancient practice of electing the Roman pontiff with the participation of the people has been transformed into an electing conclave of a special group of cardinals, a practice unknown in the early Church. It is also the case in the life of the parish and the diocese. The people are deprived of their participation in the selection of their pastors. This is not, however, all bad. The Roman Catholics are spared the many temptations that afflict those who possess the knowledge of Orthodox Christianity, because there certainly is a kind of corruption in the life of the Church. It must be noted here, however, that the Roman rite of ordination has kept one detail, alas forgotten by us, namely the laying of the hands on the candidate not only by one bishop, but by other presbyters also. The ordination is not performed only by the archbishop, but by the whole ecclesiastical assembly.

Orthodoxy has strived, and is still striving, although not always successfully, to take the middle road, avoiding one extreme appearance of Western Christianity and abstaining from excesses of another. From time immemorial, Orthodoxy has preserved the principle of electing a priest and a bishop by the people. However, it remains to be seen how this matter will be resolved by Church Historians; New Testament scholars, and canon lawyers; will they be able to demonstrate with absolute conviction the fundamentality of this or some other election system; did the Apostles, in consultation with the people, choose their priests; can Christ's words be completely ignored; "you did not chose Me, but

I chose you" (John 15:16); words which denote the choosing is to come not from below, but from above; generally speaking, does this election system conform to the spirit of the Gospel, that is, can we extract from a few factors of apostolic history general deductions; is there an undisputed advantage and an invariable correctness of choosing by the required actions of the so-called "people — guardians of piety"? All these questions cannot help but be reflected in the attitude of the priest in his parish and his relations with his flock. Understandably, this third aspect mitigates the first two extremes: Presbyterian anarchy and Latin Papism. Yet not everything in this tradition is undisputable and flawless. The participation of the people in the choosing of their pastor is not, *per se*, a bad beginning, but it does not guarantee its practice. Those people who are reared within the Church's strict framework and who are true to its canons and traditions can more or less properly exercise their right. But in the absence of these qualities, the flock's liberal tendencies for independence may well prove to be a restraint on those who do the choosing, the "people — guardians of piety," especially if the priest's character is somewhat weak.

Be that as it may, the principle of being chosen by the people, or, more to the point, the laity's participation in indicating to the authorities which candidate appears to be the more suitable, was, by and large, widely practiced in the East. The ancient Russian custom used the principle of "the prince will elevate the people." The council affirmed this statute for ordinary Churches, while palace courtiers conducted the selection of priests in the prestigious Churches. A formal note of order was issued, attesting to the desire on either side not to overstep the conditions of the agreement; this aspect brings a certain foreign spirit to the element of pastorship. It is unlikely, due to the shortage of properly prepared candidates, that it would somehow occur to the bishop to exercise his right of a veto. Under the auspices of the Holy Synod of the Russian Church, the principle of appointing the clergy by election fell into disuse and the desire for its restoration was only expressed at the workshops of the Synodal assemblies.

More recently, in the 18th and 19th centuries, the principle of the election of clergy was practiced to a certain extent in the regions of the Austro-Hungarian Empire with Orthodox populations, especially the Dioceses of Voevodina, Bukhovina, Chemowitz, and Dalmatia.

Without a doubt, some positive aspects in the election of clergy by the people may be perceived. Each person is granted the right to choose for oneself the spiritual leader and to entrust to him, and to no one else, one's conscience and one's soul. Nevertheless, in the priesthood and pastorship, the patriarchal principle of seniority holds sway. The pastor and his flock form what the Old Russian proverb called the penitent family. In a family, as well as in a patriarchal social order, a crucial element of obedience and penance has to be present. The principle of clergy election carries within itself a certain lack of humility as well as somewhat juridical and democratic elements.

It is now time to put aside these issues and turn our attention to the most important matter — ordination — its meaning and substance. The priest, whether chosen or appointed by the personal power of his future diocesan bishop, still has to face, at a certain moment of his life, this mysterious and awesome hour of ordination. Symbolically speaking, the following parallels may be drawn: election by the flock is somewhat akin to a courtship, but ordination — that is his wedding with the flock. This symbolism is fortified by common rituals and by one or another sacrament: walking around the lectern or Altar, singing the psalms ("Rejoice, O Israel," "Holy Martyrs"…) (in reverse order).[1] At this point, certain conclusions can be drawn: the union of the priest with his flock

---

[1] Editor's note: Kern here refers to three hymns that are included in both the marriage service and in the ordination service:

> O holy martyrs who fought the good fight and have received your crowns: entreat ye the Lord, that our souls may be saved.

> Glory to Thee, O Christ God
> the Apostle's boast
> the Martyr's joy
> whose preaching was the consubstantial Trinity.

is a lasting union, just as the principle of marriage; neither can be dissolved. Therefore, the transfer of a priest from one place to another should have no place in the principle of this union, as well as, or, if not to a greater extent, the transfer of a bishop from one cathedral to another. In essence, the priest is irremovable. But there is yet another, a more important characteristic to this sacrament: priesthood, as taught by Roman Catholics, is indelible. The Greek theologians held the same opinion. Metropolitan Filaret had a different view. Essentially, the grace bestowed by the bishop to perform the solemn sacrament of liturgy cannot be removed by any power on earth. To consider that any conservatory act could deprive a person of the grace of the Holy Spirit seems to be a theological aberration. Neither baptism nor priesthood are removable or indelible. Even the sin of apostasy does not erase the grace of baptism. The most frightful sin that can be committed by the priest, which leads to disenfranchisement from the Holy Orders, cannot, by itself, deprive the priest of grace. It would seem to be necessary, in case of some judicial error in defrocking a priest who is subsequently found to be innocent, to re-ordain him, which action, of course, even the strictest and most inflexible person dare not

---

Rejoice, O Isaiah! A virgin is with child, and shall have a son Emmanuel, both God and man
Orient is his name
whom magnifying we call the virgin blessed.

suggest. What should be declared as being even more frightening and blasphemous is the so-called sacramental defrocking, practiced in the Russian and Serbian churches. A well-known case of such defrocking involved Bishop Varlaam Smolensky during the reign of Emperor Alexander I. The condemned was led by the people from the chancel in full regalia, then, at the doors facing West, all the while proclaiming *anaxios* (unworthy), his priestly garments were taken off piece by piece, and as a final act, he was chased out of the temple with a rod. These proceedings bring to mind the inside-out structure of the Black Mass which was practiced during the Medieval period in the Western Church. The Greeks acknowledge the life-long loss in denying the priest to serve, but by no means do they advocate the loss of rank. As is well known, the Catholics have developed a complete set of instructions in the study of a so-called sacramental character, that is, the indelible seal of the two sacraments — baptism and priesthood.

In 1899, the Serbian Synod deprived the archpriest Milan Durić of his priestly rank for making an attempt on the life of King Milan Obrenović. He was subsequently convicted and sentenced to twenty years of hard labor. The stripping of Holy Vestments was performed in Church while proclaiming "unworthy."[1] The book of Metropolitan Michael of Serbia *Orthodox*

---

[1] Prof. G. Voskresensky, "From the Church Life of Orthodox Slavs," in *Theological Bulletin*, March 1900, p. 530.

Serbian Church in the Kingdom of Serbia[1] includes this "Rite of Expulsion From Priesthood."

With these preliminary considerations in mind, we may now turn to the main theme of this chapter—the priesthood itself. In addition to everything else mentioned in the previous chapters about the calling, pastoral gifts and the multifaceted preparation for his future service, a candidate for the priesthood should never forget about the endurance of the gift of priestly service, which separates the ordinary layman from the blessed celebrant at the Altar; the one who performs the sacrament, the theurgist, the intermediary between God and the world, who, by the grace of the Holy Spirit leads his flock to spiritual perfection, to worship. After ordination, he is no longer merely a man, but a clergyman. He is no longer the chosen one, chosen by his flock—if such choosing took place—but the bearer of grace.

The right-hand ordination by the bishop, introducing him to the parish clergy does not tear him away from the flock nor lock him into some kind of priestly caste, but organically ties him to those who from now on will be one with him.

After engaging time and again in rigorous self-examinations and being finally convinced, as far as is humanly possible, that he does not want to look back, the candidate at last decides to accept the grace

---

[1] pp. 213–215.

of priesthood, according to the rite of Melchizedek. Our pastoral theologians usually advise the candidate not to postpone the ordination for too long a time after the conclusion of his theological studies. This is probably due to the fact that each unnecessary delay does not strengthen but rather dampens the enthusiasm, brings more and newer doubts and destroys the unity of the soul. Besides, there is probably another consideration.

According to Metropolitan Anthony, God must be given all of one's fervor, to "light a whole candle in the presence of God, not offer God a good-for-nothing candle-end, spent on trivial worldly vanities." Yet, the same Metropolitan Anthony advises, as far as it is possible, to separate the time of ordination from the time of marriage. As a matter of fact, the ambience of youthful enthusiasm and passion adds little to one's ability to retain that inner self-possession, so essential for the moment of ordination and even more so for the priest's first steps into pastorship. It is time to settle down.

It may be good for the candidate to withdraw for a short time, perhaps a few days before the ordination itself and move away from all worldly concerns. Retreating into a monastery, be it ever so small and insignificant, will help the candidate to withdraw into his inner world, to pray better and with greater ease. Fasting, prayer and abstaining from all that is worldly will aid the candidate to approach the awesome hour of ordination.

The eve of ordination has arrived. The candidate fulfills all the required formalities, wastes no additional time in paying attention to the formality of his attire nor any other necessary preparations; signs his priestly oath in the conservatory, an oath which he must treat with utmost seriousness and awe; and finally, with the requisite papers from the bishop and the conservatory, he goes to his confessor, or, if there is such a one, to the confessor of the clergy for a so-called candidate's confession. This is a new and final examination of the candidate's conscience before ordination. This confession is for an entire life. Of course, each confession should be viewed as a complete confession, for at any given hour one must be prepared to face death and the judgment of God. But this confession is a particularly strict examination of all that was committed by the candidate over the span of his lifetime, things that could have been forgotten in previous confessions, or, due to human weakness even hidden and never confessed. With a reconciled conscience, a pure heart, a full awareness of his own worthlessness and imperfections, but not, however, a stylized "disparaging humility, beyond pride," yet a truly contrite heart, the candidate, in the presence of his witness, the confessor, bring his confession to God and asks God to bestow upon him the purity of the priesthood.

Through forgiveness, the signature of the confessor or by the act of the conservatory, attesting to the fact that no canonical obstacles for ordination were found, the candidate awaits the next day's ordination. St. Gregory the Theologian says in his apologetic address: "I am ashamed of others, who, with unwashed hands and unclean souls take the most holy office before they are worthy, enter the priesthood, storm into the sanctuary, push and shove around about the Holy Table, performing its office not as an example of virtue but merely as a means of making a living. Not as a service with its underlying responsibilities, but performing the duties of said office autocratically and without giving account." He further adds: "One must first cleanse himself before cleansing others, become wise before imparting wisdom, become holy before enlightening others, come nearer to God, then lead others to Him, sanctify self, then bless others."

Very often, just before ordination, those who are weak or overly judgmental, or perhaps excessively self-demanding, possessing an over-scrupulous conscience, succumb to the well-known condition of faintheartedness and the desire to run away without looking back, lest the burden they take upon themselves will prove to be overly excessive. Such a temptation deserves an answer. One must not, in these last minutes before ordination, hesitate or vacillate, remembering that a "double-minded man is unstable in all his ways" (James 1:8). For those who find these last minutes so painful and agonizing, the firm hand of the confessor, the encouraging voice of a real friend can and must supply help to the weakening conscience of the candidate. Here it is imperative to point to the grace of the Holy Spirit, "which healeth that which is feeble and fills that which is wanting."

These last hours may be safely compared to a personal Gethsemane, a temptation to forsake God. Father Sergius Bulgakov spoke about "dying" before his ordination. "It seemed as if each day was a long, drawn-out agony, bringing with it new experiences of suffering, sufferings which are impossible to describe."[1]

During these hours, a kind of self-impoverishment takes place, as if one is saving all the viewpoints and perspectives for the Kenosis of the Son of God. The priest is called upon to duplicate the priesthood of Christ, to become like Him, to begin to imitate Him in everything. In ordination, a new birth of a person takes place; the layman becomes "the new creation in Christ."

There occurs in this unique and incomparable moment of life man's commitment to obedience to Christ. The candidate proclaims the awesome vows of his special love for the Superior Pastor and the Church, uniting himself to them for eternity, not by losing self or his personality, but opening self to the mystical unity with the Body of Christ, being led and filled by His Spirit and raised into heaven.

Every moment of this solemn performance is significant and awesome; the initiations into the first stag-

---

[1] *Autobiographical Notes*, p. 41.

es of the priesthood — reader, sub-deacon, the passing for the first time through the Royal Doors, as if through some fiery barrier, walking around the Altar, accompanied by the chanting of wedding hymns, touching the Altar for the first time, the bending of knees and the sensation of the heavy brocade *omophorion* upon the head, the right-handed episcopal blessing, and perhaps the most awe-inspiring words of the bishop, spoken in an undertone into the ear of the candidate: "Raise your eyes into heaven and ask God for forgiveness of your sins and the bestowing upon you the purity of priesthood." These words, like lightening from heaven, pierce the person's soul, like a fiery sword, they cut off all the sinfulness from him, like a thunder-clap or perhaps like a "cold, thin voice," they grasp the hearer with the words of prayer: "O, divine grace, which always healeth that which is ailing and completes that which is wanting, vouch for the most devout deacon, (name) to be a presbyter; let us pray for him, and bring down upon him the Grace of the Holy Spirit."

"The most staggering," writes Father Sergius Bulgakov, "was, of course, the passing for the first time through the Royal Doors and approaching the Holy Altar. This felt as if I were passing through fire, a fire that singes, enlightens and regenerates. This was like entering into a different world, a Heavenly Kingdom. For me, this was the beginning of my new existence, my permanent home, where I have resided from that time on, even until now."

Not only are the Royal Doors now open, but the deacon's doors also, as a sign to signify the relationship with the worshipers, a closer link with the people — destined to be a more spontaneous act than other sacraments. All of this is keenly felt in the repeated *axios* during each part of priestly vesting, chanted at the Altar by the servers and the clergy, that is, by those who, with their chants, express the feeling of the people.

The final moment at last: the handing to the new priest the discos with a particle of the Holy Lamb with these words, "receive this pledge, bear its agonizing existence until the day of the Terrible Coming of Our Lord Jesus Christ." Now the new priest is no longer a mere layman, he is a theurgist and a celebrant of Sacraments. This is no longer someone who is merely bearing the title of father, but is in fact Father. He must, according to St. Gregory the Theologian, "stand with the angels, give glory with archangels, offer up the sacrifice on the rock of the Sacrificial Altar and perform the Holy Rite with Christ, recreate creation, reclaim the image of God, work in the mines of the world and above all — to be like God and create gods."

From this moment on begins not a just an existence, but a saintly life; not merely conversations, but sermons, not the feebleness of a long-standing weakling, but the boldness of Christ's friend, "forgetting those things which are behind and reaching forward to those things which are ahead" (Philippians 3:13), the Kingdom of grace, eternity and crucifixion of Christ.

APPENDIX

Two Models of the Pastorate: Levitical and Prophetic

The historical study of the mutual relations of the Old Testament Levitical and prophetic institutions does not fall within the purview of this essay. This would belong to the subject of biblical archeology and history. Thus the systematic exegesis of the relevant texts and books, both legalistic and prophetic, has no bearing on my theme. I will refer to those texts only when they can serve to substantiate the basic thoughts of my theme and shed a biblical light on what is especially relevant to these two concepts. It should be remembered that there is no part of this article and not a single mention of the Levitical name should be understood as some kind of a diminishment of this sacred Old Testament institution. It should not be forgotten that the Levites were part of a divinely established institution and any attempt to remove them from their prominent place would be a violation of something sacred.[1]

---

[1] First published in *Zhivoe predanie*, Paris: YMCA Press, 1937, and translated by Fr. Alvian Smirensky.

In this connection, it is important to make one more caveat in clarifying our theme. The expression "Levitical" and "prophetic" in the sense and in their mutual relationship used by me are not just mine. I am appropriating them from one of the most original minds of 19th century Russia, Bishop Porfirii Uspensky, who in his time was the authoritative expert on the Church. In his mind, these expressions had an especially specific meaning. They are seen not so much in their literal, biblical historical meaning as an institution for service to God, but as a special *terminus technicus* (technological term, Lat.) as a characteristic of a particular temperament, as a specific key in that service. In saying "Levite" or "prophet," I thus presume, so to say, to describe a pastoral style. A Levitical and a pastoral designation in this case is used to define specific categories of spirituality. These are not institutions of religious practice but are religious and psychological types.

Pastoral theology takes note of types of pastoral practice. For example, we make a distinction between a rural priest, an urban priest, a missionary, a teacher in a theological school, a catechist, etc. Do Levitical or prophetic approaches describe special ways of sacred service? No. A Levitical and a prophetic style of pastoral service can manifest itself in any of the above-mentioned categories. Furthermore, pastoral theology makes a distinction between good and evil pastoral activity. These are qualities of pastoral service. A question arises: is a "Levite" synonymous with a bad pastor? Not at all. A Levite can function with very deep, sincere and pure motives. We do not see a Levite as necessarily a mean, negligent, avaricious or an unworthy pastor. A Levite is not necessarily stupid, but the style of his service will still be a synonym for a certain spiritual backwardness.

It is time to raise the question: What are these types of pastoral practice? What are their substantial differences?

A Levitical type, in this special meaning, is one from a priestly caste, one who is conventional, formal, narrowly nationalistic, inert, and uncreative. In Old Testament times, the Mosaic Law priesthood was hereditary and exclusive. There were sufficiently legitimate historical precedents for this. Christ's preaching and ministry inaugurated something new. A new vine was planted. The Word of God and truth were no longer the property of a particular people but were preached to the whole world and to all creation. The God-man and High Priest Himself gave the example and opened a new way to the priesthood. He did not select His "little flock" from influential families and tribes, nor did He gather His Apostles because of their special status. Here is the beginning of the new and not hereditary priesthood. The apostles, hierarchs, Fathers and teachers of Christianity came into the Church from all walks of life to proclaim eternal life. A shoemaker and a shepherd become bishops. A refined philosopher and a lawyer become Christian apologists. Ordinary laymen become guardians of holy things and bearers of truth. No wonder the words of the Apostle Peter that Christians are "a chosen race, a royal priesthood, a holy nation, called into destiny" are so often mentioned and commented upon by the Fathers. This universal priesthood of Christians, not the hierarchical but spiritual, was frequently mentioned in the first years of the Church's life. For this reason, an exclusive priestly caste is totally out of place in Christianity.

Bishop Porfirii says: "The holy Fathers and teachers of the Church, Dionysius the Areopagite, Ignatius, Tertullian, Chrysostom, Basil the Great, Gregory and Augustine did not inherit their altars and cathedras from their fathers. Nicholas the Wonderworker, Spyridon, Lucian the presbyter and martyr did not study in the academies such as we have. There were bishops and priests in Russia long before the establishment of seminaries."[1]

Until the time when, because of historical circumstances, the priesthood locked itself into a caste, it was more free and alive. Having become locked up, it acquired and expanded its inherent deficiencies. It narrowed its path. It backed away from its flock. It unwittingly transformed itself into a clerical estate and appropriated exclusive prerogatives for itself, presuming itself to be the Church.

---

[1] *Book of My Life*, vol. 3, p. 95.

This engendered the mistaken view of sacerdotal service not as an "example of virtue but as a means of livelihood; not as a service subject to responsibility but as an authority not subject to accountability" (*Third Oration* of Gregory the Theologian). Pastors who are Levites at heart jealously preserve the exclusiveness of their caste and cannot tolerate the appearance of a priesthood outside of their caste.

A characteristic mark of the Levites is their conventional stamp. It became a problem in that caste's environment. This conventional image is very close and familiar for Russians. The strong, rooted, centuries-old Russian social establishment ensured stagnation everywhere, in every stratum of society. It was especially deeply rooted within the clerical milieu. We all remember or in any case have heard about that dense, nearly impenetrable clerical society. Who is not nostalgic for those pictures, long lost to the past and which are found nowhere in the West and not even among our Orthodox brethren in the Balkans and in the Near East? This static, dear to the heart way of life is gone. We can regret its passing. We can be nostalgic about it, but in no way can or should we artificially restore it, as if it is an essential attribute of clerical life and work. Convention is a witness of a degree of an incarnation or a manifestation of a particular spirit in life, but convention which is artificially constructed can in no way recreate the spirit of the past. For this reason, convention is sterile: it is afraid of anything new and is capable of squelching real progress, replacing the substance with form.

Thus, to presume the need for some kind of a narrowly conventional state as essential for priestly service is to sin against the very essence of the evangelical concept of the pastoral office. It is an attempt to confuse the living pastoral vocation with Levitical formalism.

Personal convention arose within the framework of a common social convention and is an essential part of it. And here is another characteristically Levitical trait. It is its subordination to specific lifestyles. Perhaps an adherence to a particular structure, a conformism with an evident social evil. Many bitter words of condemnation have already been directed by Old Testament prophets against this failing of pastors. In contrast to this, the more vivid examples of what has not been in conformance with the fallacy of the well-known social order, we find in the face of the "fiery and flaming" prophet, and the one "clothed with camel's hair and girded with a leather belt" — Elijah and John the Baptist. The earliest successors of the Apostles were of similar indifference to earthly goods and honors of this world, those about whom an early source says, "They live in their own countries but as aliens. They have a share in everything as citizens, and endure everything as foreigners. Every foreign land is their fatherland, and yet for them every fatherland is a foreign land ... They busy themselves on earth but their citizenship is in heaven. They obey the established laws, but in their own lives they go far beyond what the laws require" (*Letter to Diognetus*, V:5, 10). These were whom Chrysostom called "the angelic society" and "newly-born" (*Sermon 7* on Acts), because they still retained the purity and the fervor of the evangelical temperament. The Christian Church presented great and splendid examples of its pastors' struggles against social evils and those forms of lives followed by royalty which, on the strength of their authority and power impinged upon the sacred character of the Church. The daring defenders of the Church against such abuse contributed their names to the glorious list of the Church's witnesses and martyrs. From apostolic times until now, they serve as our inspirations and examples: Ambrose, John Chrysostom, Philip of Moscow, Arsenii Matsevich, Metropolitan Benjamin and others.

Nonetheless, at the same time, numerous other servants before the altar, positioning themselves in the service of the system and becoming submissive before secular falsehoods, became witnesses to the sad impotency of Levitism. Many people hostile to the Church frequently entertain this aberration: today's Christianity has subjected itself to the service of particular forms of State powers, a capitalistic structure, thus the Church has somehow allied itself with wealth. The poverty of apostolic times has been forgotten as well as the less-than-privileged status of the primitive Christian Church, as was the "holy poverty" of Francis of Assisi and the venerable Sergius of Radonezh. There are numerous admonitions and criticisms made by many of today's writers about this deficiency. One cannot but agree with this, and pastoral conscience does not permit one to contradict them.

It is interesting that this deficient tendency can easily and subtly operate concurrently with the most sincere and outstanding pastoral endeavor.

Great and notable ascetics, whose personal monastic, spiritual and pastoral lives were without reproach, at the same time endorsed many things within a socially evil system. They excused what was inadmissible and justified evil, thus becoming servants of what was false. A personal ascetical life was not infrequently mixed with a service to, or a political accommodation with, forces of social evil. This obscured the purity of the pastoral way by distorting it and by submitting the Kingdom of God to Caesar.

According to the Fathers, priestly service is incomparably higher than royal service (Chrysostom, *Sermon* 3, On the Priesthood) — "The worthiness of priesthood is beyond measure" (Ephraimm the Syrian, "Sermon on the Priesthood"), but throughout history it, to great distress, not infrequently lowered itself to the service of the traitorous interests of the police. Frequently, the Semitic priesthood, in their accommodation to the forms of the State's ways in order to preserve its shaky authority, actually lowered its own status in seeking protection for itself from the State. For example, this is how the missionary pastors, members of the Missionary Assembly, behaved in seeking the support of the secular armed forces against sectarians and schismatics.[1] The pastor who teaches with reliance upon punitive police powers, distorts his apostolic ministry to zero and violates the Gospel. The pastor who accommodates himself to the establishment, no matter which kind, and defends social evil, is no longer Christ's servant. "Am I now seeking the favor of men, or of God? Or am I trying to please men? If I were still pleasing men, I should not be a servant of Christ," writes St. Paul (Gal. 1:10; I Thess. 2:4–6).

The self-contained and ossified Old Testament Levitical institution of scribes gave birth to the concept of "tradition of the fathers" followed by Talmudism. It is of no purpose to think that Talmudism is an achievement of the Hebrew tradition alone. Alas! It has penetrated and has broadly spread itself into Christian religious psychology as well. It should be remembered that Christ the Savior has not so fervently remonstrated against any sin or human failing as he did against Talmudism, that legalistic, bookish approach to God. The most profound failures and distortions of the human soul found the possibility of forgiveness, but the Talmudic ossification of the

---

[1] Archbishop Anthony Khrapovitsky, *Works*, vol. II, p. 303.

Living Truth found only a bitter rebuke and severe denunciation. Why? Because this was a sign of slavery, of spiritual cowardice and a lack of faith. The Talmudist believes that one is saved through form, length of prayers, this or that potion, the quantity of olives, dates and figs, and not divine mercy. It is precisely this which kills the life of the Spirit. A true submission to the Spirit, in spirit and in truth is distorted into a dead, formalistic service, in a performance of rites and an obsession with rubrical detail. This, perhaps, is one of the more frightening particularities of the Levitical style.

As in any religious life, as well as in Christianity, there are elements which are eternal and which are transitory. The confusion of these two concepts, the canonization of transient forms, the designation of something which is simply old as something eternal and as such, immutable, is precisely a witness to this Levitical inclination towards Christian Talmudism. In the life of any religion, as long as it has not finally died, there were and will be conflicts and struggles between the two directions and trends: conservative and creative, static and dynamic, Old-Ritual-Levitical and the boldly prophetic.

In Christianity, this Talmudism is a remnant of that trend in the Church which already in the first century would creep to the surface and somehow try to grab and hold back the gradually receding Old Testament Law. The struggle between the Judaizing narrowly-legalistic attitude with the broad, universal and creative approach was not resolved at the Apostolic Council in 51 AD. It has always been present in the Church. There had always been pastors and laity who would seek their salvation in form, in the letter, in petty prescriptions of the *Ustav* [a manual prescribing minute details of liturgical rites, fasting, etc., developed in monasteries] whether this related to fasting, prayer or to something else. There was always the desire to replace the essence of the Good News, to shackle the spirit, to elevate sacrifice over mercy, to strain at the gnat of the *Ustav* and swallow the camel.

Everything that is being described is by no means and not even in a small measure, an attack on the holiness of tradition and the legacy from the past, since Christianity is a living reality and not something doctrinaire or bureaucratic. But it is alive only in the Church, only where grace and heritage from the past abide. Without a loyalty to the past, Christianity is incomplete. Thus, by the way, it must be pointed out that the desire to turn back to absolute primitive Christianity, to toss aside the centuries-old and living experience of the Church is unsavory and essentially incorrect. "Back to Christ" means to turn away the whole of the Church's tradition. This would be a dissipation of all the riches in the Church's treasure house: those mystical and ascetic experiences, liturgical theology, iconography, etc. In other words, it would be an impoverishment or a rejection of Christianity. The

Church and her life do not reflect only primitive Christianity, no matter how tempting it may be for us. That life reflects the fullness of the total experience of the humanity of God in all the ages. Yet, the rejection of every approach to that tradition and experience which is Talmudic or formalistic is in no way a contradiction of, or an irreverence towards that love and loyalty towards the Church's tradition and experience.

The formalistic and Talmudic approach is precisely what kills the living heritage of the grace-filled Church. Talmudism and the primacy of form, shackles the creative impulse, does not adapt to the eternally revealed Truth and practically forbids the Church to live. This Talmudism impinges not only on the parochial, liturgical and administrative lives of the Church. It goes further. It does not think. It does not live by the Spirit. It refuses to acknowledge theological creativity. It is like the people of the Old Testament who told the prophets, "Do not prophesy" (Amos 2:12) or "Prophesy not to us what is right" (Isaiah 30:10). For them, revelation has come to a stop. They say, "Truth, which is necessary for our salvation, has been revealed in full. The Church can exist and live on the wealth of its spiritual capital accumulated over the ages. Everything has been given to us in the Gospel and the Fathers. Anything else comes from evil and is not needed."

Here one forgets that thought cannot avoid thinking. Man's mind, according to St. Gregory the

Theologian, cannot avoid moving towards the Great Mind, that man has not been created just to be a passive recipient of prepared and ready-made truths from on high, but that he himself participates in Revelation, himself seeks and creates. Creativity is one of the attributes of man's spirit which reflects the image and likeness of God. New life continues to be created in the Church.

The pastor-Levite is afraid of this in the Church. He wants to put a stop to its life-flowing source. He himself does not think. He is afraid to think and forbids others to think. He is completely immersed in a deep and placid hibernation. He is oblivious to any of the crying contemporary questions raised by a dangerously sick, suffering and disturbed humanity. Nothing disturbs him in his spiritual hibernation. He is unaware of anything that goes on around him and only wants one thing: how to remain in this dormant and inert state as long as possible while justifying himself in that by this he is somehow "guarding" something.

The pastor-Levite likewise wants to settle on the ossified forms of the expressions of faith. He speaks in some kind of a pseudo-classical preacher's jargon, larded with Church-Slavonic expressions which are difficult for the faithful to understand. He is afraid of the living, commonly understood language. The Levitic school and the manual of ecclesiastical rhetoric in the spirit of the homilies of hierarchs such as Filaret and Innocent forbid him from speaking otherwise.

The pastor-Levite introduces the Talmudic spirit in the celebration of divine services. The form and the letter are more valuable to him than the sincere, prayerful attitude coming from the heart. He is afraid to make of divine service something more comprehensible and accessible to the faithful. He is a slave of the rooted, petty patterns in the sacred ritual, for example: the reading of the Word of God in a well-known stereotype, with rolling vocal cadences, in an attempt to impress the listeners with his lower and higher registers which may be completely incomprehensible to the faithful. He loves pomp and theatrical nuances and believes these to be the sense and meaning of Orthodox Church service. The spirit of Talmudism tries to justify itself with its love for ritualistic traditions, but that love does not go beyond an empty formalism: it becomes a ritual for the sake of ritual and external esthetics at the price of comprehending the prayer's meaning. The New Testament Talmudism is mistaken if it thinks that form and ritual engenders a spirit of prayer. If the prayerful spirit is absent, if the priest does not have the prayer within him, then no book of rubrics can create a prayerful atmosphere. The book of rubrics can be compared here to "the way we do things." As such, it generates a particular attitude but in itself it is nugatory. It is nothing more than a monument or a record of a particular way of prayer and its development as well as a regulating symbol of liturgical life and practice, but of itself it creates nothing nor can it bring to life a fading light.

The Levitical spirit also confines itself into narrowly-nationalistic frameworks. It overlooks that salvation has been proclaimed to all, that in the Gospel there is neither Jew nor Greek, that there is no place for Chauvinism in the Church. Becoming a slave to forms of social structure, canonizing and justifying man-made superstructures and barriers, it is likewise enslaved to national fetishes. The idea of a truly catholic Church embracing all tribes and peoples is alien to it. He did not discern in the miracle of the fiery tongues at Pentecost how "all began to speak in strange tongues with strange doctrines, by the strange commands of the Holy Trinity," how in the Divine symphony of tongues all the people give one mighty accord to the glory of God's name. He cannot rise above his ethnic, provincial interests and tastes. He still crawls about within the boundaries of Old Testament concepts and is incapable of rising to the level of the whole world. This spirit of pagan love only towards his own people and language stands in the way of the Levite's ability to pray in Church if the singing there is not according to one's accustomed style and not even in one's own language. Here, that narrowly-ethnic spirit at one time made the Greeks burn Arabic service books and Bulgarian antimensions while the Slavs burned the Greek ones. The whole idea of the universal oneness of the Church is alien for the

Levite. He is quite pleased with what he has. He makes no effort to learn about the life and faith of his co-religionist brothers or to pray with them with one mouth and one heart, even if in different languages. He is not disturbed by the estrangement of Christians and the scattering of the flock. The problem of uniting the scattered bits and pieces of Christianity does not concern him nor does he think about it. The sight of the present rendering of Christ's robe leaves him indifferent. He is not disturbed that the Church remains shattered in the face of militant atheism. Divided along dogmatic questions, among tribes and nations, along the differences of the calendar and of customs, according to jurisdictions and names of hierarchs, the Church today stands as a reproach to all and especially to pastors. It is especially sad and painful to see this division of Christ's seamless robe where it would seem there should be no place for it: in Jerusalem's holy places, at the Lord's sepulcher, at the foot of trembling Golgotha, where at one time the Roman soldiers dared not to tear Christ's robe. The pastor, who is indifferent to this, who is not sick at heart, and who does not fervently pray for the union of all has failed to overcome that Levitical spirit within himself. He has not been able to rise to the level of Christ's High Priestly prayer, "that they may all be one" (Jn. 17:20).

The priesthood of the Levitical tradition, in other words, has fallen into a deep slumber. It fell asleep even before the Divine Logos ascended upon the earth and it has neither awakened nor was it capable of hearing how that Logos, having become incarnate, proclaimed a new Truth and a new commandment for all people and most certainly and primarily for the pastors, who are called to carry out that commandment.

What then is a "prophet" as a type and a role model for a pastor in the Church?

It is not what the Church designated and canonized as a specific type of righteous individuals in the Old Testament. Although the term is taken from the Bible, it is given a somewhat different meaning, more akin to the types found in early Christian times. A prophet in that sense is not one who foretells the future. He is a bearer of the creative spirit who does not hesitate along the path of his pastoral activity, always hungers and thirsts for communion with the Source of righteousness, sensitive to everything that takes place in the world, not compromising with the deeply-rooted evil and falsehood no matter by what authorities of this world they may be sanctioned. These are pastors who are conscious of being priests of God in the Highest, of the Living God, themselves living expressions of the faith. It is those pastors who sense and experience the tragedy of Christianity and of their own calling.

An Old Testament prophet was rarely a priest (Ezekiel 1:3; Jeremiah 1:1; 1 Chron. 24:20). These were two parallel institutions of the religious establishment. But the New Testament priest must also be a prophet in the spirit of his pastoral calling. He cannot be otherwise. The Old Testament Levite becomes a priest as a birthright. A prophet is called directly by God. Neither the privilege of caste nor the accomplishments of the forbears could elevate him to the level of his service. "I am no prophet, nor a prophet's son," they said (Amos 7:14).

The Old Testament prophet denounced the shortcoming of priests, kings and people by his flaming rhetoric and his lifestyle. He was sent from on high as a kind of a corrective for the inadequate examples of the priesthood. The priest of the New Testament, as a prophet, must constantly hear that Divine voice as a corrective within himself.

The Old Testament prophets were directly called from all levels of society and from different places (kings, shepherds, etc.) and were inspired by the Holy Spirit. Christ's pastors receive that same grace of the Holy Spirit at their ordination, "which always heals what is infirm and completes what is wanting." If those ancient prophets heard the voice of God and communed with God, then the New Testament prophet-priest communes regularly with the Lord Himself in the sacred mystery of the Eucharist. Does he not hear the Lord's voice? The ancient prophet was not afraid to open his ears and his heart to the knowledge and discernment of the Divine Truth. Must the New Testament prophet-priest be afraid of this, he who is given no lesser measure of the grace of that same Holy Spirit, no matter how awesome, out-of-place, and disturbing that Truth may be? The prophet of old preached the idea of moral renewal and an internal re-birth (Isaiah 1:10; 6:7; Hosea 6:1; 12:3, 6, etc.), condemned social evil and the injustices of the powerful, stirring his people and priests awake. He was an uncompromising guardian of truth. Must not the New Testament prophet and priest be no less than that? Has he not been called to carry out his service towards the mystical transfiguration of the world?

In the Old Testament, God gave Moses the institution of the priesthood and the ritual of sacrifice. The Levites were the custodians who carried out those prescriptions. The prophets in their merciless chastisement of the Levites did not condemn the ritual and sacrifice. They rose up against the manner of carrying out these rituals and sacrifices. They fulminated against the priests who "... have done violence to my law and profaned what was sacred to me. They make no distinction between the sacred and common" (Ezekiel 22:26), "you priests who despise my Name" (Malachi 1:6); "... her priests give direction in return for a bribe" (Micah 3:11) ; "... who care only for themselves" (Ezekiel 34:2); and "... they feed on the sin of my people, they are greedy for their iniquity" (Hosea 4:8). Thus, the New Testament pastor must constantly engender within himself the prophet's relationship towards sacrifice, prayer and the rules of the Church and not the perfunctory Levitical treatment of the Sacred.

The Old Testament prophets were servants of all the people. Naturally, they stood on the level of the national Hebrew understanding of revelation and the idea of the Divinely chosen Israel. One must not forget that there also were prophets who rose above this narrowly national level. The Lord called some of them for service beyond the confines of the Hebrew people (Prophet Jonah) and opened up broader horizons for them (Zechariah 7:12–13). But they were incapable of rising to the idea of service to the whole of mankind. This became the lot of the New Testament pastors. Here the pastor must not dare to turn back to the Old Testament concept and lock himself within nationalistic boundaries. The task of the Christian pastor is broader, and he must sacrifice his ethnicity, his customs and his prejudices in favor of broader, universal service. Patriotic tendencies, no matter how exalted they may be, cannot be above the evangelical, universal aims. Nationality must be subordinated to the universal, Christian trans-nationality. If the pastor is unable to do this, he is once again a slave to Levitical atavism.

Bishop Porfirii said: "In all of Europe, there is a great spiritual crop failure. The mediocrity and the deep hibernation of spiritual forces replaces the stimulation and the flow of gifts in the sphere of certainty, goodness, beauty and truth. Russia is exhausted by spiritual poverty. Where are our prophets who would nurture Russia with inspiring words, inclined towards faith, poetry and the beauty of the spiritual world? Where are our prophets who, in God's name and that of the Gospel, would preach freedom to the enslaved? Where are the apostles?" (*Book of my Life*, vol. 3, pp. 238–239).

But the prophetic spirit and style is so uncommon in the general level of the spiritual bourgeoisie. They seem like harsh discordant sounds. They disturbingly force themselves into the quiet murmur of comfortable, serenely happy and comfortable Christianity. Such people are looked upon as utopian simpletons. So, the question arises: Is prophetic service possible today? Is it not a specific variant of the Old Testament or early Christian religious practice?

If one views religious life as something completely fixed and immobile and sees Christianity simply as an accumulation of completed maxims and pastoral calling as merely the task of preserving traditions and established rites and forms, then the prophetic inclination and a fervent spirit is but an anachronism and any effort to attain this is a futile, pitiful and dangerous attempt to return to a life which has long ago gone by the wayside.

But if Christianity is not dead, if the Church is alive even now, if our liturgy still has that force as it had in the early days of the Church's life, if the divine, miraculous grace is still efficacious through the priest and he sanctifies nature, restores the sick, has power over evil, blesses and transforms this world obscured by sin — then we cannot be dead in our faith nor dare be other than fervent in spirit. In such a case, we pastors cannot but be inspired with the spirit of Elijah, Isaiah, the Forerunner John the Baptist, the Apostle Paul and the prophets of the *Didache*. I repeat: to be a prophet does not mean only to foretell the future. It means to be bold and vibrant before God. It means not to make peace with the reigning evil. It means to awaken the dormant religious consciousness, to be responsive and deeply sensitive to all problems which are so burdensome to mankind. If the spirit of the apostles and prophets is dead within us, then we are merely like a caste of Levites and priests offering fiery sacrifices.

Sensing a cooling of spirit in their Christianity and the ossification of empirical forms in their Church, the Apostle writes to the Thessalonian community: "Do not despise prophesying" (I Thess. 5:20). In that prophetic spirit, he saw the boldness of faith, the deposit of authentic service, and he wanted to see the same in his heirs and successors in service to the Incarnate. He was not mistaken in his concerns. Just as in times past Israel told its prophets: "Do not prophesy truth to us, tell us flattering things, have illusionary visions" (Isaiah 30:10; Amos 2:13) so the spirit of bold service before God gradually began to diminish. Form began to triumph over substance, and only a pale shadow of the Gospel remained. They began to forget and fear that prophetic spirit. To be sure, it is much less disturbing without it. There is no need to be fervent. One need not seek. One can find contentment within the comfortable confines of established ways. In this, there is a tremendous temptation. The early Christian community in the poignancy of its religious inspiration, continued to live in the spirit of prophetic service and was not afraid of it. *The Didache* allowed "the prophets to give thanks as much as they wanted to," that is literally "to make eucharist," to pray liturgically. St. Justin Martyr, the philosopher, likewise testifies that the priests presided and prayed liturgically as much as they could, i.e. as much as they were inspired with strength. This shows that they clearly saw and felt the authentic power of faith in their religious inspiration. This was like a criterion of the authentic religious life. There was nothing false or artificial or distorted in this kind of a spiritual path.

In one of his *Orations* (42, the "Farewell") about the miracle of Pentecost, St. Gregory Nazianzus makes an excellent characterization of the state of the spirit in the just-enlightened and grace-filled Apostles: "This was the power of the spirit and not the frenzied mind." All service of the Christian Church was centered here. The Christian as such, and especially the pastor, must be filled with the force of the Spirit, that prophetic Spirit. He cannot be otherwise. John Chrysostom was not afraid to say: "We become prophets when God reveals to us that what the eye has not seen nor the ear heard (I Cor. 2:9). In the baptismal font, you become king, priest and prophet" (*Sermon* 3 on II Corinthians).

It probably will not be out of place to say that there has not been a more crucial and responsible time for Christ's Church since apostolic times to this day. The signs of catastrophe and the image of the apocalypse of our era are sufficiently clear for everyone except those who are still blind.[1] The Lord does not tolerate and strongly condemns a lukewarm faith (Rev. 3:16). In our times especially, there can be no dead faith, dormant spirituality or deafness with respect to what is taking place in the world. There is a shifting of immense strata of what once was firm and stable for centuries. Mobs arise against the Church, but large caravans of lost strangers also find their way back. The prophet's words stand vividly before today's pastor: "Behold the days are coming, says the Lord God, when I will send famine on the land; not a famine of bread, nor a thirst for water, but of hearing the words of the Lord" (Amos 8:11), and he must realize that to quench that hunger and thirst demands a priesthood of a prophetic type. They must be fully armed prophetically to meet today's challenges in carrying out their service. There are many pastoral paths before us and each one of these is blessed and each one

---

[1] Editor's note: This essay was published in 1937.

demands zealous workers. The path taken depends on individual capabilities and inclinations as well as upon the needs of the Church which sends them to be her representatives. But no matter how they will carry out their task, they must do this in the spirit of the Good Shepherd, not looking backward to the secure, peaceful, stable Levitical service, but bearing in mind the tragic circumstance of our times and daring to meet the challenge.

But first of all, do not dampen within yourself that religious pastoral inspiration. Go forward following the steps of the prophets and the Apostles. Do not fear that youthful fire burning in them. Do not quench it. Do not be tempted to cuddle up to the traditional comforts. Do not fall for aesthetics at the cost of spirituality. Do not be afraid, being inspired by the fervent Spirit, not to appear as a contemporary type. Be utopian. Be a fool. Don't be tempted by the comforts of the mediocre spiritual bourgeoisie. Remember the words of St. Gregory Nazianzus which I cited above, and serve not with a frenzied mind but with the power of the Spirit.

"Do not quench the Spirit nor do away with prophesy." We tried to bring out in this essay just what the prophetic spirit is and what it means to be a prophetic and not a Levitical pastor.

www.ingramcontent.com/pod-product-compliance
Lightning Source LLC
Chambersburg PA
CBHW032120090426
42743CB00007B/409